GRADE 2

READING

SPECTRUM

Columbus, Ohio

Index of Skills

Reading Grade 2

Numerals indicate the exercise pages on which these skills appear.

Table of Contents

A Big Tuna Trading Company, LLC/J.R. Sansevere Book

Send all inquiries to: School Specialty Publishing, 8720 Orion Place, Columbus OH 43240-2111

ISBN 0-7696-8082-8

8 9 10 11 12 13 GLO 13 12 11 10 09

WELCOME TO CRITTERVILLE!
Spider
Frog
Grasshopper
Mouse
Little Critter
Little Sister
Dad
Kitty
Mom
Blue
Gator
Bat Child
Gabby
Bun Bun
Tiger
Maurice
Molly
Malcolm

Trouble With Blue

Read to see why Little Critter has to clean up the garden.

Little Critter saw his mom standing at the door of his room. "Mom, why are you holding a shovel?" asked Little Critter.

"I think you will need it, Little Critter," said Mrs. Critter.

"Why?" asked Little Critter.

"Come downstairs and see," said Little Sister, poking her head inside.

Little Critter followed his mom and sister out to the yard. The garden was a mess!

"Oh, no!" said Little Critter. "Blue's been digging again."

"Little Critter," said Mrs. Critter, "I think Blue needs to be trained."

"You're right, Mom," agreed Little Critter. "I better train him. It shouldn't be hard. Blue is smart."

Blue barked and wagged his tail. Little Sister giggled as she looked at Blue's muddy paws. "He doesn't look very smart to me!"

Name ______________________________

Thinking Skills

Directions: Circle the word that best completes each sentence about the story. Then, write the word in the blank.

1. Mom was holding a ______________.

   shovel　　　shoe

2. Little Critter and his mom went out to the ______________.

   yard　　　yarn

3. Little Critter thinks Blue is ______________.

   small　　　smart

Reading Skills

Directions: Write a sentence that describes the picture on this page.

____

____

Language Skills

Directions: Write a pronoun that could replace the underlined word or words.

1. <u>Little Critter</u> wants to train his dog. ______________

2. <u>Mom</u> said the garden was a mess. ______________

3. Put <u>the shovel</u> away.

   ____

A Talk With Blue

Read to see what Little Critter tells Blue.

Little Critter and Little Sister helped their mom all afternoon. They filled the holes that Blue had dug. They planted new flowers. Little Critter tried to water the garden, but Blue wanted to play.

"Get out of the way, Blue!" yelled Little Critter.

Blue didn't listen. He just barked and shook himself. Water flew everywhere, getting Mom and Little Sister both very wet. They went inside to dry off.

Little Critter shook his head. "Blue, we need to talk," he said. He climbed into Blue's doghouse. Blue climbed in after him. "Blue, you have to stop digging," said Little Critter. "And you have to learn how to listen. I don't want you to get into more trouble. You're a smart dog. I just know you can be good."

Little Critter hugged his dog. Blue gave Little Critter a big, wet kiss.

"I hope that means yes," said Little Critter.

Name ______________________________

Thinking Skills

Directions: Circle the word that best completes each sentence about the story. Then, write the word in the blank.

1. Little Critter and Little Sister ____________ Mom.

   talked helped barked

2. They planted new ____________.

   trees water flowers

3. Blue got everyone ____________.

   muddy happy wet

4. Little Critter ____________ his dog.

   kissed hugged petted

Reading Skills

Directions: Write a sentence that tells about Blue.

____

____

Directions: Write a word from the story that rhymes with each word below.

1. book ____________
2. hug ____________
3. walk ____________

Blue Gets Out

Read to find out where Blue goes.

The next day, Little Critter's mom asked him to get the mail.

"Sure, Mom," answered Little Critter. He walked down the path to the mailbox. He unlatched the gate, opened the mailbox, and got the mail. On his way back to the house, he looked at the mail.

Just then Blue saw the open gate. He dashed past Little Critter and ran out of the yard. "Blue, come back!" cried Little Critter. "Here, Blue!" Little Critter dropped the mail and chased his dog.

Blue jumped over a fence. Little Critter jumped over the fence. Blue crawled under some bushes. Little Critter crawled under the bushes. He could not catch Blue. Little Critter ran through his neighbors' yards and called for Blue. He ran right into Mrs. Crabtree.

"I'm sorry, Mrs. Crabtree. I was just looking for. . ." Little Critter tried to explain.

Mrs. Crabtree frowned. "I think I know just who you are looking for," she said.

Name ______________________________

Thinking Skills

Directions: Answer the questions about the story.

1. Why was the gate open?

____

____

2. Tell one thing that Blue did after he ran through the gate.

____

____

3. Why was Mrs. Crabtree frowning?

____

____

Reading Skills

Directions: Number the sentences **1**, **2**, and **3** to show what happened first, next, and last in the story.

_____ Blue ran through the open gate.

_____ Little Critter chased Blue.

_____ Little Critter looked at the mail.

Mrs. Crabtree's Roses

Read to see why Little Critter has to check his piggy bank.

"Your dog has dug up my prize-winning roses," said Mrs. Crabtree. She pointed to her yard. There were red flower petals everywhere.

"I'm really sorry, Mrs. Crabtree," said Little Critter. "Blue just likes to dig. Don't worry. I promise it won't happen again." Blue lay down at Little Critter's feet and put his head on the ground. "See, Mrs. Crabtree. Blue is sorry, too," added Little Critter.

"Those roses were my pride and joy," said Mrs. Crabtree. "You will have to pay for them. I think twenty dollars is about right."

"Okay, Mrs. Crabtree," said Little Critter. "I'll pay you back as soon as I can."

Little Critter walked slowly home with Blue.

"Blue, this is just the kind of trouble I was talking about," said Little Critter. "Twenty dollars is a lot of money. I better go check my piggy bank."

Name ____________________

Thinking Skills

Directions: Answer the questions about the story.

1. Why was Mrs. Crabtree angry?

____

____

2. What did Little Critter tell Mrs. Crabtree?

____

____

Reading Skills

Directions: Write the words from the story in **ABC** order.

1. bank ____________
2. yard ____________
3. red ____________

Language Skills

Directions: Circle each **action word** below.

dog walk money
dig say

Little Critter's Friends Help Out

Read to find out how Little Critter's friends try to help.

The next day, Little Critter was playing with his friends, Maurice, Molly, Gabby, and Tiger. He told them all about Blue and Mrs. Crabtree's roses. He told them about the twenty dollars.

"Boy, was she mad," said Little Critter. "And I only have $2.23 in my piggy bank. Mom says I have to earn the rest."

"I have a dollar you can have," said Tiger. He pulled a crumpled dollar bill from his pocket.

"You can have my allowance," added Gabby. "I was only going to buy candy anyway." Gabby handed Little Critter some coins.

"We can help, too," said the twins, Maurice and Molly, at the same time.

"Thanks a lot," said Little Critter. "I bet this will be enough."

Little Critter counted the money. It came to $5.27.

"You need lots more than that," said Gabby. "But don't worry. I think I know just how we can earn the rest."

Name ______________________________

Thinking Skills

Directions: Answer the questions about the story.

1. What is the main idea of the story?

____

____

____

2. How much money did Little Critter have in his piggy bank?

____

3. What are your ideas to earn the extra money?

____

____

Reading Skills

Directions: Write two words that rhyme with each word from the story.

1. rest ____________ ____________
2. roses ____________ ____________
3. think ____________ ____________
4. same ____________ ____________
5. bill ____________ ____________
6. bet ____________ ____________

Gabby's Idea

Read to see what the friends plan.

A little while later, Gabby came over to Little Critter's house with a big sign. It read:
Lemonade — five cents a cup.

"My idea is to open a lemonade stand," said Gabby. "Then we can sell lemonade to make money."

"Great idea," said Little Critter. "I'll make the lemonade."

"Maurice and I will get paper cups," said Molly.

"I'll bring a table and chairs," added Tiger.

"Meet you here in half an hour," said Gabby.

Little Critter hurried to make the lemonade. The directions said to use two scoops of lemonade mix, but Little Critter used four. He wanted to make sure it tasted really good.

Little Critter carried the heavy pitcher outside. "We're ready for business!" he said.

Name ____________________

Thinking Skills

Directions: Answer the questions about the story.

1. How much lemonade mix did Little Critter use?

____

____

2. What did Maurice and Molly bring?

____

____

3. How do you think the lemonade will taste?

____

Reading Skills

Directions: Write two words from the story that have each vowel sound.

1. Long a ________ ________
2. Short i ________ ________
3. Short a ________ ________

Directions: Write a word from the story that rhymes with each word below.

1. mouse ______________
2. take ______________
3. fix ______________

More Trouble for Blue

Read to see what happens at the lemonade stand.

Little Critter and his friends sat at the lemonade stand. Blue lay on the ground at Little Critter's feet and chewed on Little Critter's shoelaces.

Just then Su Su walked by with her dog, Fifi. Fifi had yellow ribbons in her curly gray fur. She smelled like perfume.

"Do you want some lemonade, Su Su?" asked Little Critter. "It's only five cents a cup."

"Okay," said Su Su.

Suddenly, Blue bounded over to Fifi and began to sniff her. The two dogs started to play. Blue ran to the garden and began to dig. Fifi pulled on her leash, trying to follow him.

"Stop that right now, Fifi!" ordered Su Su. Fifi wouldn't listen. She pulled so hard, Su Su lost hold of the leash. Fifi ran after Blue.

"Here, Fifi!" cried Su Su.

"Here, Blue!" called Little Critter.

The dogs wouldn't listen. They just kept playing in the dirt.

"Fifi is a purebred poodle," Su Su yelled at Little Critter. "And I'm training her for the dog show. I knew I shouldn't let her play with a mutt, like your dog."

Su Su stomped off and dragged Fifi out of the dirt. Her ribbons had come untied. Her gray fur was all brown.

"Oh, no, Blue," said Little Critter. "More trouble."

Name ______________________________

Thinking Skills

Directions: Answer the questions about the story.

1. Do you think that Blue and Fifi were having fun? Why?

____

____

2. Why was Su Su angry?

____

____

Reading Skills

Directions: Write the word that best completes each sentence about the story.

walked	pulled	sniffed

1. Blue ______________ Fifi.
2. Su Su ______________ with Fifi.
3. Fifi ______________ on the leash.

Language Skills

Directions: Write the root word for each word below.

1. training ______________
2. started ______________
3. pulled ______________
4. trying ______________
5. chewed ______________
6. playing ______________
7. smelled ______________
8. dragged ______________

A Sale

Read to see who is the first customer at the lemonade stand.

Little Sister came outside to see how business was going. She laughed when she saw muddy Blue licking the dirt off his paws. "That dog is a mess," said Little Sister. "Have you sold any lemonade yet?"

"No," said Little Critter.

"Too bad," said Little Sister. "I bet it'll take you forever to make twenty dollars."

Just then Mrs. Smith, the letter carrier, came walking toward them. "Lemonade sounds great on this hot day," said Mrs. Smith. "I'll take two cups, please."

"See," said Little Critter. He proudly poured two cups.

"You're our first customer," added Gabby.

Mrs. Smith gave Little Critter two nickels. Then she took a sip of lemonade. She puckered her lips.

"How's the lemonade?" asked Little Sister.

"Very–um–tasty," said Mrs. Smith.

Tiger put the nickels in a cup. He shook the cup. The nickels jingled.

"We'll have the twenty dollars in no time," said Little Critter.

Name ____________________

Thinking Skills

Directions: Answer the questions about the story.

1. Who is Mrs. Smith?

____

____

2. What did Mrs. Smith give to Little Critter?

____

____

3. Do you think Mrs. Smith liked the lemonade? Why or why not?

____

____

____

Reading Skills

Directions: Number the sentences **1**, **2**, and **3** to show what happened first, next, and last in the story.

_____ Mrs. Smith asked for two cups of lemonade.

_____ Little Sister wondered how business was going.

_____ Mrs. Smith gave Little Critter two nickels.

Directions: Write the words from the story in **ABC** order.

muddy ______________

lemonade ______________

cups ______________

tasty ______________

dollars ______________

A Long Way to Twenty Dollars

Read to see how much money Little Critter makes at the lemonade stand.

Little Critter and his friends worked at the lemonade stand all afternoon. Mr. and Mrs. Critter each bought a cup of lemonade.

"Very tangy, Little Critter," said Mr. Critter.

After that, Tiger's brother bought a cup. Maurice and Molly's cousins bought three cups. Gabby's dad bought a cup, too.

"Let's count the money," said Little Critter. He and Tiger counted all the coins in the cup. The total only came to forty-five cents.

"That's a long way from twenty dollars," said Little Sister. "Maybe you should raise the price."

"We just have to be patient," said Little Critter. "I'm sure we'll sell lots more lemonade."

At sunset, they had only sold two more cups. Little Critter and his friends were hot and tired.

"Don't worry, Little Critter," said Gabby. "We'll think of something."

"Maybe we should go into town tomorrow," said Tiger. "I bet we'll find a way to make money there."

Little Critter smiled and thanked his friends. "See you tomorrow," he said.

Name ______________________________

Thinking Skills

Directions: Answer the questions about the story.

1. What is the main idea of the story?

____
____
____

2. What did Mr. Critter say about the lemonade?

____
____
____

3. What did Tiger think they should do?

____
____
____

Reading Skills

Directions: Write the word that best completes each sentence about the story.

bought	counted	thanked

1. Mr. and Mrs. Critter ____________ some lemonade.
2. Little Critter ____________ his friends.
3. They ____________ the coins in the cup.

Directions: Write a word from the story that means the **opposite** of each word below.

1. none ____________
2. cold ____________
3. short ____________

Gabby's New Idea

Read to find out about Gabby's new plan for Blue.

The next day, Little Critter and his friends went into town. Little Sister and Blue came, too. Along the way, they passed a notice for the dog show.

"I know!" exclaimed Gabby. "Let's enter Blue in the dog show. First prize is twenty-five dollars!"

"I don't know, Gabby," said Little Critter. "Blue needs a lot of training."

"Don't worry," said Gabby. "I have a book about training dogs."

Little Sister giggled. "I hope it's a really good book," she said.

"Blue can do it," said Tiger.

"No problem," agreed Maurice and Molly.

"Dog training will start this afternoon," said Gabby. "We'll work really hard with Blue every day. You'll see. He'll be just as well-behaved as Fifi in no time!"

"Woof! Woof!" barked Blue.

Name ____________________

Thinking Skills

Directions: Answer the questions about the story.

1. What is the main idea of the story?

____

____

2. Why does Gabby want to train Blue for the show?

____

____

____

3. Do you think that Gabby can train Blue? Why or why not?

____

____

Reading Skills

Directions: Write a sentence that describes the picture on this page.

____

____

____

Language Skills

Directions: Write a contraction from the story that stands for each pair of words below.

1. we will ____________
2. do not ____________
3. let us ____________
4. it is ____________
5. he will ____________
6. you will ____________

Little Critter's News

Read to find out if Little Critter's mom and dad like the news.

Little Critter ran home with Little Sister and Blue. "Mom! Dad!" he called, as he opened the door. "Guess what? We're going to enter Blue in the dog show! First prize is twenty-five dollars. If Blue wins, then I can pay Mrs. Crabtree the money I owe her."

"Good idea," said Mr. Critter. Mrs. Critter thought so, too.

Little Sister shook her head. "How are you going to train him if he never listens?" she asked.

"Learning to listen is part of the training, Little Sister," said Mrs. Critter. "We have to remember Blue is just a puppy. He can learn."

Suddenly, Blue started whining. The Critters saw a puddle on the floor right next to him.

"Little Critter, I think Blue needs to go out," said Mr. Critter.

"He sure has a lot to learn," said Little Sister.

Name ______________________

Thinking Skills

Directions: Answer the questions about the story.

1. How much money is the first prize worth in the dog show?

____

____

____

2. What will Little Critter do with the money?

____

____

____

3. What did Mrs. Critter say about Blue?

____

____

____

4. Why was Blue whining?

____

____

____

Reading Skills

Directions: Write a sentence that tells about each picture below.

1. ______________________

____

2. ______________________

____

Directions: Write a word from the story that rhymes with each word below.

1. cart ____________
2. pins ____________
3. cook ____________
4. main ____________

Blue's First Lesson

Read to see how much Blue has to learn.

Gabby, Maurice, Molly, and Tiger all came over to Little Critter's house to help train Blue. Gabby brought her dog training book, *Dog Training the Easy Way.*

"I don't think there is an easy way to train Blue," said Little Sister. Maurice and Molly laughed.

"Lesson One: Teach Your Dog His Name," Gabby read aloud. "Always use your dog's name when you ask him to do something."

"Here, Blue!" Gabby called. Blue jumped up and licked Gabby's face. "You try, Little Critter," she said, as she wiped her face.

"Here, Blue!" said Little Critter. Blue jumped on Little Critter and knocked him down. "You try, Tiger," he said.

"Here, Blue!" shouted Tiger. Blue bounded toward him and grabbed the baseball out of his hand. Then he ran for the garden with the ball in his mouth.

"We're finished with Lesson One," said Gabby. "Blue definitely knows his name."

"That's about all he knows," said Little Sister.

Name ______________________________

Thinking Skills

Directions: Answer the questions about the story.

1. What is the main idea of the story?

____

____

____

2. What was Lesson One about?

____

____

Reading Skills

Directions: Write each group of words from the story in **ABC** order.

1. face ______________
   about ______________
   knows ______________
   try ______________
2. jumped ______________
   think ______________
   try ______________
   down ______________
3. him ______________
   he ______________
   his ______________
   here ______________

Language Skills

Directions: Circle the nouns in each row.

1. hand baseball use ask
2. train house think laugh
3. know easy book garden
4. face mouth dog jumped

Too Much Food

Read to see why Blue has a big belly.

One morning, Little Sister woke up Little Critter. "You better come see what your dog did," she said.

Little Critter followed Little Sister to the kitchen. There was dog food everywhere. Blue had torn open the bag and helped himself.

"Blue, you've eaten way too much," said Little Critter. "You don't look good."

Just then, there was a knock at the door. It was Gabby. "Hi, Little Critter. Are you ready for the next dog training lesson?" she asked.

"He's ready," said Little Sister. "But Blue's not." She pointed to Blue. He was lying on the floor with his stomach sticking out.

"He ate too much," said Little Critter. "Now he's so full he can't move."

"We'll have the next lesson when Blue feels better," said Gabby.

"I hope he's better before the dog show," said Little Critter.

"Maybe he could win the prize for the biggest belly!" said Little Sister.

Name ______________________________

Thinking Skills

Directions: Answer the questions about the story.

1. What is the main idea of the story?

____

____

____

2. Why wasn't Blue ready for the next lesson?

____

3. What kind of prize might Blue win?

____

____

Language Skills

Directions: Write a contraction from the story that stands for each word or words.

1. he is ____________
2. we will ____________
3. you have ____________
4. do not ____________

Directions: Follow the example to complete the chart.

big	*bigger*	*biggest*
small		smallest
	taller	
short		

Walking on a Leash

Read to see what Blue does at his next lesson.

"Now that Blue feels better, he can learn to walk on a leash," said Gabby.

Little Critter and his friends went to the Critterville Park. Little Sister came, too.

"Lesson Two: Walking on a Leash," Gabby read aloud from her book. "Use the word 'heel' to tell your dog to walk beside you."

"Heel, Blue," said Little Critter. Blue wanted to play with the leash instead. He walked around Little Critter.

"Heel, Blue," tried Tiger, walking over to Little Critter.

"Stop, Tiger," said Gabby. "Only Little Critter should give Blue commands."

But it was too late. Blue ran toward Tiger, tangling the leash around Little Critter. Little Critter tripped and fell onto the grass. He knocked into Tiger. Tiger fell on top of Little Critter. Blue stood on top of Tiger and barked.

Maurice, Molly, and Little Sister laughed. They helped Little Critter and Tiger to their feet.

"Some dogs may need more practice than others," Gabby read.

Little Sister giggled. "I think Blue is one of those dogs!"

Name ______________________________

Thinking Skills

Directions: Answer the questions about the story.

1. Where does the story take place?

____

2. What is the main idea of the story?

____

____

3. What do you think will happen next?

____

____

Reading Skills

Directions: Circle the word that best completes each sentence about the story. Then, write the word in the blank.

1. Little Critter and his friends ____________ to the park.

   went sent want

2. Tiger fell on ____________ of Little Critter.

   hop tap top

3. Gabby ____________ aloud from her book.

   head need read

4. Blue needed to learn how to ____________.

   feel heel sit

Directions: Write a word from the story that rhymes with each word below.

1. day ____________
2. talking ____________
3. wood ____________
4. tell ____________
5. feel ____________
6. letter ____________

The Missing Slipper

Read to find out what happened to Mr. Critter's slipper.

"Little Critter," called Mr. Critter. "Have you seen my other slipper?"

Little Critter helped his dad look for the slipper. First, Little Critter looked in his toy box. Then he looked in the kitchen cupboards. He looked under the sofa. He looked in Little Sister's closet. He could not find the slipper anywhere.

"Did you check the doghouse?" whispered Little Sister.

Little Critter hoped Blue didn't have the slipper. He stuck his head in the doghouse. There was Blue, chewing on Mr. Critter's slipper.

"Bad dog," said Little Critter. He took the slipper from Blue. Maybe his dad wouldn't notice.

"Dad! Dad!" called Little Critter. "I found your slipper."

"Great," said his dad until he saw his slipper. It was soggy and it had holes in it. "It looks like Blue ate my slipper for breakfast," said Mr. Critter.

"Sorry, Dad," said Little Critter.

Little Sister laughed. "I wonder if Lesson Three will teach Blue not to eat slippers!"

Name ______________________________

Thinking Skills

Directions: Answer the questions about the story.

1. What is the main idea of the story?

____

____

2. What question did Mr. Critter ask Little Critter?

____

____

3. What happened to Mr. Critter's slipper?

____

____

Reading Skills

Directions: Write the root word for each word below.

1. chewing ______________
2. whispered ______________
3. holes ______________
4. looked ______________

Language Skills

Directions: Write an adjective to describe each noun below.

1. ______________ slipper
2. ______________ doghouse
3. ______________ sofa
4. ______________ kitchen
5. ______________ toy

Mrs. Crabtree Stops By

Read to find out what Mrs. Crabtree has to say about the dog show.

Gabby came to train Blue every afternoon. No matter how hard Little Critter and his friends worked, Blue still did not listen.

One afternoon, when Little Critter was working with Blue, Mrs. Crabtree came over. "Sit, Blue!" said Little Critter. Blue kept rolling around in the grass instead.

"Hello!" said Mrs. Crabtree. She looked at Little Critter, then at Blue, and back again. "What are you kids up to?"

"Hi, Mrs. Crabtree," said Little Critter. "We're training Blue for the dog show. First prize is twenty-five dollars. If Blue wins, then I can pay you for the roses."

"Really?" asked Mrs. Crabtree, looking down at Blue. He was digging a hole at her feet.

Little Critter smiled at Mrs. Crabtree. He put his arms around Blue.

"Good luck!" said Mrs. Crabtree, frowning.

"Good luck!" repeated Little Sister. "You're definitely going to need it!"

Name ______________________________

Thinking Skills

Directions: Answer the questions about the story.

1. What is the main idea of the story?

____

____

2. What did Little Critter tell Mrs. Crabtree?

____

____

Reading Skills

Directions: Write a sentence that tells about each picture below.

1. ______________________________

____

2. ______________________________

____

Language Skills

Directions: Circle the word that best completes each sentence. Then, write the word in the blank.

1. Gabby __________ to train Blue every afternoon.

   come　　came　　coming

2. Blue was __________ a hole at her feet.

   dig　　digs　　digging

Fifi Shows Off

Read to see why Blue howls at Fifi.

Another afternoon during dog training, Su Su walked by with Fifi. Fifi was wearing a sparkly new collar and a blue sweater.

"Guess what?" said Gabby. "We're training Blue to enter the dog show, too."

"Well, you'll never win," said Su Su. "Fifi is the smartest dog in Critterville. She knows lots of tricks. Watch this." Su Su turned to Fifi. "Sit, Fifi," said Su Su. Fifi sat. "Stay, Fifi," said Su Su. Fifi stayed. "Roll over, Fifi," said Su Su. Fifi rolled over. "Speak, Fifi," said Su Su. Fifi began to yap.

Blue did not like the sound. He began to howl. Fifi started howling, too.

Little Critter and Gabby laughed. Tiger howled along with Blue and Fifi. Maurice and Molly clapped for the dogs' song. Su Su covered her ears. "Let's go, Fifi," said Su Su, "before you learn any more bad habits."

"Let's try that again," said Gabby. "Sing, Blue!" Blue howled.

"Good dog, Blue!" said Little Critter.

"At least he knows one trick," said Little Sister.

Name ______________________________

Thinking Skills

Directions: Answer the questions about the story.

1. What is the main idea of the story?

____

____

2. What did Blue do when Fifi began to yap?

____

____

3. What part of the story did you like best? Why?

____

____

Language Skills

Directions: Write each verb in the past tense by adding the ending **ed**. The first one is done for you.

1. train trained
2. stay ______________
3. roll ______________
4. howl ______________
5. turn ______________

Directions: Circle the nouns in each sentence.

1. Fifi was wearing a sparkly new collar and a blue sweater.
2. Fifi is the smartest dog in Critterville.
3. Su Su covered her ears.

Dizzy Blue

Read to see what all the noise is about.

"How are the dog training lessons going?" asked Mr. Critter at dinner that night.

"Great," said Little Critter. "Blue is really learning to behave."

Suddenly, the family heard crashing sounds. They headed for the living room. A chair was lying in the middle of the floor. Next to it was Blue, spinning round and round, chasing his tail.

"Stop, Blue!" cried Little Critter.

Blue kept spinning. He knocked over a lamp. The lamp knocked some books off the bookcase. The books fell on the table. The table crashed to the floor. Mrs. Critter covered her eyes.

Mr. Critter put his arms around Blue. Finally, Blue stopped spinning. He looked very dizzy. He wobbled from side to side.

"Easy, Blue!" said Mr. Critter.

Little Sister helped Little Critter clean up the mess. It took them so long, Little Critter missed "Super Critter," his favorite TV show.

"Stop looking so mad," said Little Sister. "Blue will learn — someday."

Name ______________________________

Thinking Skills

Directions: Answer the questions about the story.

1. What did Little Critter say when his dad asked him about the dog training lessons?

____

____

2. Why was Blue dizzy?

____

____

Reading Skills

Directions: Write the word that best completes each sentence about the story.

suddenly	bumped	wobbled

1. Blue __________ from side to side.
2. __________, the family heard a crash.
3. Blue __________ into the chair.

Directions: Write each group of words from the story in **ABC** order.

1. learn ______________
   lessons ______________
   lamp ______________
2. stopped ______________
   side ______________
   spinning ______________
3. crashed ______________
   chased ______________
   covered ______________

Little Critter Has the Blues

Read to see how Little Critter's mom helps.

Little Critter walked slowly up the stairs to his bedroom. He threw the door open with a bang. He grumbled as he put on his pajamas. Then he got into bed and pulled the covers over his head.

"Little Critter," said his mother quietly. "Is everything okay?"

"No," said Little Critter. His voice sounded funny from under the covers.

"What's wrong?" asked Mrs. Critter.

Little Critter pulled down the covers. "Blue is never going to act right," said Little Critter. "He's never going to win the dog show. I'll never be able to pay for Mrs. Crabtree's roses."

"Never say never, Little Critter," said Mrs. Critter. "You're doing your best, and I'm very proud of you. You just have to be patient. Blue will learn. I'm sure everything will be okay." Then she gave Little Critter a big hug.

"Thanks, Mom," said Little Critter. "You always make me feel better."

Name ____________________

Thinking Skills

Directions: Answer the questions about the story.

1. Why was Little Critter upset?

____

____

2. Who helped Little Critter feel better? How?

____

____

3. What are some things that you do to feel better when you are sad?

____

____

Reading Skills

Directions: Look at the picture of Little Critter's room. Write a sentence that describes it.

____

____

____

Directions: Write a word from the story that rhymes with each word below.

1. bunny ____________
2. song ____________
3. pairs ____________
4. bread ____________
5. know ____________

Blue Joins the Picnic

Read to see what Blue wants to eat.

The next evening, the Critter family had a picnic. They invited Gabby's family and Tiger's family. Maurice and Molly's family came, too. Mrs. Critter made potato salad and coleslaw. Gabby's dad made brownies. Tiger's mom and dad brought over a volleyball set. Maurice and Molly's parents made two kinds of cupcakes. Mr. Critter cooked hot dogs and hamburgers on the grill.

Little Critter and his friends played volleyball until it was time to eat. Blue played, too. He hit the ball with his head. He even got the ball over the net once. All the kids laughed.

"Who's ready for a hot dog?" asked Mr. Critter. "Come and get it!"

"I am," said Tiger. Mr. Critter picked up a hot dog with a fork. Before the hot dog made it to Tiger's plate, Blue jumped up and grabbed it in his mouth. Everyone laughed.

"No, Blue!" cried Little Critter.

"Sorry, Tiger," said Mr. Critter. "I'll get you another one."

"You did say come and get it," said Little Sister to Mr. Critter. "I guess Blue thought you meant him, too."

"I better take him to his doghouse for a while," said Little Critter. "We don't want to run out of hot dogs."

Name ______________________________

Thinking Skills

Directions: Answer the questions about the story.

1. Where does the story take place?

____

____

2. What did Dad cook for the picnic?

____

____

3. What do you think will happen next?

____

____

Reading Skills

Directions: Write the word that correctly completes each sentence about the story.

family	grabbed
hit	took

1. The Critter __________ had a picnic.
2. Blue __________ the ball with his head.
3. Blue __________ the hot dog.
4. Little Critter __________ Blue to his doghouse.

Directions: Write the word or words from the story that begin with each consonant blend.

1. br __________ __________
2. pl __________ __________
3. gr __________ __________

Shake, Blue

Read to see how Mr. Critter helps train Blue.

The next day, Little Critter and his friends met in the backyard for Blue's lesson. "Today we're going to teach Blue how to shake hands," said Gabby. She pointed to her dog training book. It showed a dog holding out his paw to a boy who was shaking it.

"How are you going to make Blue do that?" asked Little Sister.

"First, we have to show him how," said Gabby. She shook Little Sister's hand. Then Tiger and Little Critter shook hands. Maurice and Molly shook hands. Blue wagged his tail and barked.

Gabby took Blue's paw and said, "Shake, Blue." She did this three times. Then she told Little Critter to try. "Let Blue give you his paw by himself," she said.

Little Critter said, "Shake, Blue." Blue laid down on the ground. "Come on, Blue," said Little Critter. "Sit." Blue sat up. Before Little Critter could ask for his paw, Blue jumped on him.

Just then Mr. Critter came outside. He was holding something in his hand. "I think this might help," he said, handing the package to Little Critter. "Reward Blue with a hot dog when he does something right."

Gabby said, "Shake, Blue." Then she took his paw. Little Critter quickly gave Blue a piece of hot dog. Blue gobbled it down. After that, Little Critter asked Blue to shake. Blue stuck out his paw.

"Good dog!" cried Little Critter and all his friends. Little Critter gave Blue another piece of hot dog.

"That dog will do anything for a hot dog!" said Little Sister.

Name ______________________________

Thinking Skills

Directions: Answer the questions about the story.

1. What did Gabby want to teach Blue?

____

____

____

2. After reading this story, do you think Blue will win the dog show? Why or why not?

____

____

____

Reading Skills

Directions: Circle the word that best completes each sentence. Then, write the word in the blank.

1. We're going to __________ Blue how to shake hands.

   take teach tear

2. Blue wagged his __________ and barked.

   train take tail

3. Little Critter quickly __________ Blue a piece of hot dog.

   game gave gate

Language Skills

Directions: Write a pronoun from below to replace the underlined words.

He	They	She

1. <u>Maurice and Molly</u> are friends with Little Critter. __________

2. <u>Blue</u> is learning new tricks.

   ____

3. <u>Gabby</u> brings her dog training book each day. __________

Lunch With Mrs. Crabtree

Read to see why the Critters invite Mrs. Crabtree for lunch.

"I have an idea," said Mrs. Critter one afternoon.

"What?" asked Little Critter and Little Sister.

"I think we should have Mrs. Crabtree over for lunch," said Mrs. Critter.

Little Critter and Little Sister both looked at their mom in surprise. "Mrs. Crabtree?" said Little Sister.

"Why?" asked Little Critter.

"Because she is our neighbor and our friend," answered Mrs. Critter.

"She won't be my friend," said Little Critter. "Because of Blue."

"That's not true," said Mrs. Critter. "Anyway, maybe Mrs. Crabtree will like Blue better if she gets to know him."

"Or maybe not," said Little Sister, giggling.

"I can make my famous peanut butter and pickle sandwiches," said Little Critter.

"Yuck!" said Little Sister. "Mrs. Crabtree would like jelly and potato chip sandwiches better."

"What about tuna fish?" said Mrs. Critter. "Everyone likes tuna fish!"

Name ______________________________

Thinking Skills

Directions: Answer the questions about the story.

1. What does Mrs. Critter want to make for lunch?

____

____

2. What does Little Sister want to make for lunch?

____

____

Reading Skills

Directions: Number the sentences **1**, **2**, and **3** to show what happened first, next, and last in the story.

____ Little Critter doesn't think Mrs. Crabtree will be his friend.

____ Mrs. Critter wanted to make tuna fish sandwiches.

____ Mrs. Critter had an idea.

Directions: Write the word that best completes each sentence about the story.

idea	sandwiches
friend	everyone

1. We will have ____________ for lunch.
2. Mrs. Critter told them her ____________.
3. ____________ likes tuna fish.
4. She won't be my ____________.

Blue Makes Friends

Read to see how Blue tries to be friends with Mrs. Crabtree.

Mrs. Crabtree came for lunch the next day. Mrs. Critter made tuna fish sandwiches. She served them with potato chips and pickles. Mr. Critter made an apple pie for dessert. Everyone ate at the kitchen table. Blue sat quietly next to Mrs. Crabtree.

"Thank you so much for inviting me," said Mrs. Crabtree.

"I'm glad you could come," said Mrs. Critter.

"We're sorry about your roses," said Mr. Critter. "You know, Little Critter is working hard to train Blue. He's hoping to pay for your new roses very soon."

Just then Blue ran out of the kitchen. He came back with Little Sister's doll in his mouth. He dropped the doll next to Mrs. Crabtree.

"I see Blue knows how to carry things," said Mrs. Crabtree.

Everyone laughed. Little Critter hoped Blue would keep behaving, but Blue ran out of the room again. This time, he came back with Little Critter's pajamas in his mouth. He dropped them next to Mrs. Crabtree. After that, he came back with a baseball glove, a teddy bear, and a towel. Blue sat down and looked up at Mrs. Crabtree.

"I think Blue is trying to be your friend, Mrs. Crabtree," said Little Critter.

"He can be my friend, as long as he doesn't dig up my new roses!" said Mrs. Crabtree.

Name ______________________________

Thinking Skills

Directions: Answer the questions about the story.

1. What did Blue bring to Mrs. Crabtree?

____

____

____

2. How do you think Mrs. Crabtree feels about Blue now?

____

Reading Skills

Directions: Write two words that rhyme with each word below.

1. lunch ________ ________
2. came ________ ________
3. roses ________ ________
4. how ________ ________
5. back ________ ________
6. keep ________ ________

Directions: Write a sentence that describes the picture on this page.

____

____

____

Perfect Dogs

Read to see what Little Critter watches on TV.

Little Critter and Little Sister watched a dog show on TV. They saw beautiful dogs do many tricks. The owners walked their dogs around a ring. The judges made notes about each dog. None of the dogs were digging, howling, or snatching hot dogs. They sat when their owners said "sit." They walked nicely when their owners said "heel." "Those dogs are perfect," said Little Sister. "Just like Fifi. I bet Su Su wins the $25 first prize."

"Blue," said Little Critter, "watch these dogs. Maybe you can learn something." Blue wasn't interested. He was busy chasing his tail.

Little Critter imagined the dog show. Blue listened. He sat. He heeled. He rolled over. He was perfect. He didn't even need hot dogs. Everyone clapped for Blue and Little Critter. The judges said Blue was the smartest dog they had ever seen. They put the first prize ribbon on Blue. Little Critter won the $25.

Little Critter's dream ended when he heard Blue barking. Little Critter and Little Sister ran to the window. Blue was sitting on the table and howling. Little Critter and Little Sister did not know why Blue was barking. There was nothing outside.

Little Sister laughed at Blue. She said, "Blue's sure not a show dog yet!"

Name ____________________

Thinking Skills

Directions: Answer the questions about the story.

1. What television show did Little Critter and Little Sister watch?

____

____

2. What did Little Critter imagine?

____

____

3. What was Blue doing?

____

____

4. What do you think Blue was howling about?

____

____

____

____

Reading Skills

Directions: Write a sentence that tells about each picture.

1. _______________

2. _______________

3. _______________

Language Skills

Directions: Write the root word for each word below.

1. laughed _______________
2. clapped _______________
3. digging _______________
4. howling _______________
5. nicely _______________

Little Sister Speaks Up

Read to find out what Little Sister says to Su Su.

Day after day, Little Critter worked with Blue. Gabby always brought her dog training book. Maurice and Molly always brought hot dogs for Blue. Blue was learning little by little. Tiger cheered Blue on. Even Little Sister became hopeful for Blue.

One afternoon, Su Su walked by with Fifi. Fifi was wearing a fancy blue polka-dot scarf.

"You're still trying to train that mutt?" asked Su Su. "He's too wild to be in a dog show."

Little Sister got mad. "Just because your dog is Miss Perfect doesn't mean you can make fun of Blue," she said.

Su Su just laughed. "We'll see who wins first prize," she said. Then she and Fifi walked away with their noses in the air.

"I want Blue to win just to make Su Su mad!" said Little Sister. Blue sat up and gave Little Sister his paw. "Maybe Blue can win the...." But Little Sister never finished her sentence. Blue jumped on her lap and licked her face. "Blue!" she cried. "Show dogs don't do this stuff!"

Name ______________________________

Thinking Skills

Directions: Answer the questions about the story.

1. Why was Little Sister mad at Su Su?

____

____

2. Why did Little Sister want Blue to win?

____

____

3. How would you describe Fifi?

____

____

Reading Skills

Directions: Number the sentences **1**, **2**, and **3** to show what happened first, next, and last in the story.

_____ Su Su and Fifi walked away.

_____ Blue put his paw out to Little Sister.

_____ Su Su wondered why Little Critter was still training Blue.

Language Skills

Directions: Write an adjective to describe each noun below.

1. ________________ scarf
2. ________________ friends
3. ________________ prize

A Surprise for Blue

Read to see what Mr. and Mrs. Critter give Blue.

That night, Little Critter and Little Sister were sitting in the living room. They were taking turns brushing Blue. Blue was busy chewing a bone. Mr. and Mrs. Critter came into the room. Mrs. Critter was holding something behind her back.

"We have a surprise for Blue," said Mr. Critter.

Mrs. Critter put a package in front of Blue. He sniffed it. Then he went back to his bone. Little Critter and Little Sister opened the package. Inside was a bright red collar with Blue's name on it.

"Blue can wear this to the dog show," said Mr. Critter. "We're proud of you for working so hard with him. He's really learned a lot."

Mrs. Critter said Blue would look very handsome in his new collar.

"Thanks," said Little Critter. "Blue sure has learned a lot."

Just then Blue stood up. He tried to dig a hole in the carpet. He wanted to bury his bone.

Little Sister said, "He hasn't learned to stop digging yet!"

Name ____________________

Thinking Skills

Directions: Answer the questions about the story.

1. What did Mr. and Mrs. Critter give to Blue?

____

____

2. What did Blue do at the end of the story?

____

____

Reading Skills

Directions: Write the word that best completes each sentence about the story.

package		back
collar	bone	hard

1. Little Critter put the new ____________ on his dog, Blue.
2. Blue wanted to bury his ____________.
3. Mr. and Mrs. Critter said that Little Critter had worked ____________.
4. Little Sister helped open the ____________.
5. Mrs. Critter was hiding something behind her ____________.

Language Skills

Directions: Write two sentences. Use one verb below in each.

dig	jump

1. ____________________

____

2. ____________________

____

A Haircut for Blue

Read to see where Blue goes.

The dog show was the next day. The Critter family wanted to take Blue to get his hair cut. They climbed into the car, but Blue would not get in. Blue did not want to go.

"Come on, Blue!" said Little Critter. He and Little Sister tried to put Blue in the car. Blue jumped out of their arms and ran into the garage.

Mr. Critter got some hot dogs. Blue followed the smell of the hot dogs. Soon he was on his way to get a haircut.

In the waiting room, Blue hid under the chairs.

"My dog is not happy about getting a haircut," Little Critter told the dog groomer.

"Don't worry," said the dog groomer. She took Blue's leash. "He'll be just fine." She held out a treat and Blue followed.

When Blue was finished, the dog groomer brought him out. Blue was shiny clean and his fur was cut short. He smelled like flowers.

"Blue, you look like a show dog!" exclaimed Little Critter.

Name ______________________________

Thinking Skills

Directions: Answer the questions about the story.

1. What is the main idea of the story?

____

____

____

2. How did Mr. Critter get Blue to go to the groomer?

____

____

Reading Skills

Directions: Number the sentences **1**, **2**, and **3** to show what happened first, next, and last in the story.

_____ Blue hid under the chairs.

_____ Blue looked like a show dog.

_____ Blue did not want to go to the groomer.

Language Skills

Directions: Write three words from the story that have the sound of **sh**. Then, write three words of your own that have the sound of **sh**.

1. ______________________________

2. ______________________________

3. ______________________________

1. ______________________________

2. ______________________________

3. ______________________________

Another Bath

Read to see why Blue needs another bath.

Blue did not stay clean for long. When the Critter family got home, he raced out of the car. He headed right for the garden. Blue dug and dug. Dirt flew everywhere.

"It looks like Blue needs another bath," said Mr. Critter.

Little Critter looked at his dog and sighed. "I love you, Blue, but I wish you could stay clean for a little while."

"Don't worry, Little Critter," said Little Sister. "I'll help you give him another bath."

First, Little Critter and Little Sister hosed Blue off in the yard. Then they carried him upstairs to the bathroom. They shut the door so Blue couldn't run away. Little Critter filled the tub with warm water. Little Sister added some doggie shampoo. Blue wasn't happy.

"Let's scrub!" said Little Sister. They scrubbed the mud off Blue's face. They washed his paws. Blue splashed. He tried to jump out of the tub. Little Critter held Blue while Little Sister washed him.

When Blue was clean, they dried him off. Then, they put a T-shirt on him to keep his fur clean.

"Blue, you're not leaving the house until the dog show," said Little Critter. "No more digging today!"

Name ______________________________

Thinking Skills

Directions: Answer the questions about the story.

1. Where did Blue go first when he came home?

____

2. What did Little Critter and Little Sister do with Blue?

____

____

3. How do Little Critter and Little Sister plan to keep Blue clean?

____

____

____

Reading Skills

Directions: Write the word that best completes each sentence about the story.

headed	scrubbed	tried

1. Blue ______________ for the garden.
2. Blue ______________ to jump out of the tub.
3. They ______________ the mud off Blue's face.

Language Skills

Directions: Write the past tense of each verb below. Remember to double the final consonant. The first one is done for you.

1. scrub scrubbed
2. pat ______________
3. pop ______________
4. beg ______________

The Dog Show

Read to see what the show dogs do.

The next morning, Little Critter put the new collar on Blue. He took off the T-shirt. Then he said, "Blue, I know you can be the winner." The Critter family got Blue into the car with no problems. They drove to the park.

Many people were already at the park to watch the dog show. Little Critter's friends were there to cheer for Blue.

"Good luck, Blue!" said Gabby and Tiger.

Maurice and Molly said, "We brought some hot dogs, just in case."

Little Critter watched the other dogs. He began to get nervous. Blue was number eight. After a while, Su Su and Fifi took their turn. Fifi wore a pink sweater with a yellow bow. She did all her tricks without any mistakes. Su Su smiled proudly when Fifi was finished.

The next dog took his turn. He was a beagle named Scout. Scout's owner had Scout sit, heel, speak, and roll over. Scout stood up on two legs and danced. Then he did a back flip. Finally, Scout carried a flower to the judges. Everyone clapped for Scout, even Su Su. It was Blue's turn next. Little Critter headed to the ring.

Mr. and Mrs. Critter wished Little Critter good luck.

Tiger and Little Sister shouted, "Go, Blue! Blue is number one!"

Name ______________________________

Thinking Skills

Directions: Answer the questions about the story.

1. What is the main idea of the story?

____

____

2. What did Scout do?

____

____

____

3. Which dog do you think will win? Why?

____

____

____

____

Reading Skills

Directions: Write the word that best completes each sentence about the story.

mistakes	flower
watched	cheer

1. Little Critter's friends were there to __________ for Blue.
2. Little Critter __________ the other dogs.
3. Scout carried a __________ to the judges.
4. Fifi did not make any __________.

Directions: Write a word from the story that rhymes with each word below.

1. kicks __________
2. slumber __________
3. pegs __________
4. know __________
5. dinner __________

Blue's Turn

Read to see what happens when Little Critter shows Blue.

Little Critter walked Blue around the ring. Little Critter was nervous. He had a funny feeling in his stomach. The judges told them to begin. Little Critter hoped Blue would listen.

"Sit, Blue," said Little Critter. Blue sat. "Good dog!" said Little Critter. "Shake, Blue." Blue gave his paw to Little Critter. "Good dog!" said Little Critter again.

Suddenly, Blue began to sniff. He tugged on the leash and pulled Little Critter around the ring. He sniffed and sniffed, his nose to the ground.

"Stop, Blue!" cried Little Critter, but Blue would not listen. He started to dig a hole. Everyone at the show laughed. Little Critter knew he wouldn't win first prize.

"No, Blue!" yelled Little Critter just as Blue dug something up. It was an old metal box. The judges ran over to see.

One of the judges opened the box. Inside were many large, gold coins. "This dog has found a treasure," exclaimed the judge. "These are stolen coins. I believe they were taken from the Critterville Bank many years ago. Everyone thought the coins were gone for good. This dog is a hero!"

"Hooray for Blue!" cried Little Critter and all his friends.

Name ______________________

Thinking Skills

Directions: Answer the questions about the story.

1. What tricks could Blue do?

____

____

____

2. What did Blue find?

____

____

____

3. What did the judges call Blue? Why?

____

____

____

4. Where did the treasure come from?

____

____

____

5. What do you think will happen next?

____

____

____

Reading Skills

Directions: Write four sentences. Use one word from below in each sentence.

sniffed	hoped
opened	laughed

1. _______________________

____

2. _______________________

____

3. _______________________

____

4. _______________________

____

Directions: Write each group of words from the story in **ABC** order.

1. funny ____________
   feeling ____________
   first ____________
   friends ____________

2. listen ____________
   leash ____________
   laughed ____________
   large ____________

Blue the Hero

Read to see how Blue becomes famous.

Scout won first prize, Fifi won second, but Blue was a hero. The gold coins Blue had found were stolen in the Great Critterville Bank Robbery. The bank gave Little Critter a $25 reward. People from the newspaper came to take pictures of Blue and Little Critter and their friends.

The reporter asked lots of questions about Blue. Little Critter told him they had been training him for weeks.

"I was in charge of the lessons," Gabby said, "because I have this great dog training book." She held it up for the reporter to see.

"We could never stop him from digging, though," added Tiger.

"He loves to dig," said Molly.

"Almost as much as he loves hot dogs," put in Maurice.

"This dog has an excellent sense of smell," said the reporter. "This time his digging made him a hero. We'd like to put a story about him on the front page."

Little Critter and his friends all smiled for the camera. Little Sister was very proud.

"I always knew that dog would be famous!" she said.

Name ______________________________

Thinking Skills

Directions: Answer the questions about the story.

1. What did the bank give to Little Critter?

____

____

2. What did Little Critter and his friends tell the reporter?

____

____

____

Reading Skills

Directions: Number the sentences **1**, **2**, and **3** to show what happened first, next, and last in the story.

_____ Little Critter and his friends smiled for the camera.

_____ The bank gave Little Critter a $25 reward.

_____ A reporter from the newspaper came to see Little Critter.

Directions: Write three sentences. Use one word from below in each sentence.

reward	proud	famous

1. ______________________________

____

____

2. ______________________________

____

____

3. ______________________________

____

____

A Party for Blue

Read to see who comes to celebrate with Blue.

The Critter family had a party for Blue. There was cake, ice cream, and, of course, hot dogs. The whole neighborhood was invited, including Su Su, Fifi, and Mrs. Crabtree.

"I'm sorry that Fifi didn't win first prize," said Little Critter.

"Next year, we will," said Su Su. "I'm teaching Fifi how to search for buried treasure." All the friends laughed.

"Blue is a hero," said Mrs. Crabtree to Little Critter. "Please bring him and your friends to my house tomorrow. I want to talk to you." Little Critter wondered what Mrs. Crabtree wanted.

He was glad he had the reward money to pay for the roses.

When the party was almost over, a long, shiny black car drove up. The Mayor of Critterville stepped out. He said, "I am looking for a dog named Blue." Little Critter was so surprised he just stood there. Then he brought Blue over to the mayor. "I have a special medal for the hero of Critterville. Thank you, Blue, for finding the lost gold coins from the Critterville Bank Robbery." The mayor hung a medal around Blue's neck.

Everyone cheered. "Woof! Woof!" barked Blue.

Name ____________________

Thinking Skills

Directions: Answer the questions about the story.

1. Why do you think Mrs. Crabtree wants to talk to Little Critter and his friends?

____

____

____

2. Describe the party for Blue.

____

____

____

3. Why did the mayor of Critterville come to the party?

____

____

____

Reading Skills

Directions: Write two sentences. Use one word from below in each sentence.

mayor	hero

1. ______________________________

____

____

2. ______________________________

____

____

Directions: Write two words that rhyme with each word below.

1. gold ________ ________

2. bring ________ ________

3. cake ________ ________

4. bank ________ ________

5. black ________ ________

Mrs. Crabtree's Idea

Read to see what Mrs. Crabtree tells the friends.

The next afternoon, Little Critter, Little Sister, Blue, and their friends went to see Mrs. Crabtree. They found her in her garden.

"Here's the money for your new roses," said Little Critter, holding out the reward money.

Mrs. Crabtree shook her head. "You keep it, Little Critter," she said. "I know how hard you and your friends worked to earn money for my new roses. I know about your lemonade stand. I know that is why you entered the dog show. There is another way you can repay me, though."

"How?" asked Little Critter.

"By helping me plant my new roses!" answered Mrs. Crabtree with a smile.

Little Critter was happy. "Guess who can dig the holes?" he said.

"Blue!" yelled all his friends.

Little Critter and his friends helped Mrs. Crabtree all afternoon. Blue dug the holes, and Little Critter and Gabby planted the roses. Maurice and Molly pulled weeds. Tiger painted Mrs. Crabtree's fence. Little Sister swept the sidewalk and porch. When they were finished, Mrs. Crabtree made lemonade for everyone.

Name ______________________________

Thinking Skills

Directions: Answer the questions about the story.

1. What is the main idea of the story?

____
____
____

2. What did Mrs. Crabtree ask Little Critter to do for her?

____
____

3. What did Mrs. Crabtree do to thank everyone?

____
____
____

Reading Skills

Directions: Look at the picture on this page. Write two sentences that describe the picture.

1. ______________________________
____
____

2. ______________________________
____
____

Directions: Circle the word that best completes each sentence about the story. Then, write the word in the blank.

1. Little Critter and his friends __________ Mrs. Crabtree.

   hugged helped hurt

2. Blue dug holes in the __________.

   group garage ground

3. Maurice and Molly __________ weeds.

   planted pulled played

4. Little Sister __________ the porch.

   swept swiped swam

5. Tiger __________ the fence.

   picked planted painted

Sweet Dreams

Read to see why everyone is happy.

Mrs. Crabtree thanked Little Critter and his friends for all their hard work. She was very happy about her rose garden. Her whole yard looked beautiful. "Thank you, too, Blue," she said and petted him. "You're a good dog."

"Good-bye, Mrs. Crabtree!" said all the friends.

Little Critter and Little Sister headed home. "I'm glad Mrs. Crabtree is our friend," said Little Critter. "I think she even likes Blue now."

"I think you're right," said Little Sister.

"Woof! Woof!" barked Blue.

After dinner, Little Critter went out to the doghouse. He brought Blue some dog food and some fresh water. They sat inside the doghouse together. "You know what, Blue?" said Little Critter. "You're the best dog in the whole wide world!" Little Critter yawned and put his arm around Blue.

Soon, Little Critter and Blue were fast asleep. Little Critter dreamed of gold coins and roses. Blue dreamed of hot dogs and digging.

Name ______________________

Thinking Skills

Directions: Answer the questions about the story.

1. How do you think Mrs. Crabtree feels about Blue now?

____

2. What did Little Critter tell Blue?

____

____

3. What did Little Critter and Blue dream about?

____

____

____

Language Skills

Directions: Write the past tense of each verb below.

1. say ______________
2. look ______________
3. bark ______________
4. dream ______________
5. sit ______________
6. is ______________
7. thank ______________
8. pet ______________

Directions: Write three sentences. Use one of the verbs that you wrote above in each sentence.

1. ______________________

____

____

2. ______________________

____

____

3. ______________________

____

____

Packing Up

Read to find out what Little Critter packs for his visit.

One evening, the Critter family was eating dinner. Little Critter was playing with his mashed potatoes. Little Sister was rolling peas on her plate.

"Children, eat your food properly, please. Remember your good manners," said Mrs. Critter.

Just then the telephone rang. Mr. Critter answered. "Hello, "Grandpa," Mr. Critter said. "That sounds like a wonderful idea. Yes, we can drive out tomorrow morning."

Mr. Critter said, "Little Critter, Grandma and Grandpa would like to have you visit the farm for a week. Would you like that?"

Little Critter jumped out of his seat. "Yes! I'll go pack right now!"

Little Critter ran upstairs and found a bag to pack. He packed his racing car, his cowboy boots, his Super Critter costume, his toy trains, and his teddy bear.

He called downstairs. "Mom, will my bicycle and skateboard and football helmet fit in the car?"

Mrs. Critter came into Little Critter's room. "Little Critter, did you pack your toothbrush, socks, underwear, and pajamas?"

"Oops, guess I forgot about those things," said Little Critter.

Name ______________________

Thinking Skills

Directions: Answer the questions about the story.

1. What is the main idea of the story?

____

____

2. Why was Little Critter packing?

____

____

3. What did Little Critter forget to pack?

____

____

____

4. What else do you think Little Critter should pack?

____

Reading Skills

Directions: Write a sentence that describes the picture below.

____

____

____

Directions: Write the word that best completes each sentence about the story.

bicycle	toothbrush	
eating	visit	packed

1. The Critter family was __________ dinner.
2. Would you like to __________ the farm for a week?
3. Little Critter __________ his teddy bear.
4. He forgot to pack his __________.
5. Will my __________ fit in the car?

A Farm Is a Busy Place

Read to see what Little Critter wants to do at the farm.

Mrs. Critter helped Little Critter pack his bag. She said, "Choose two of your favorite things to bring." Little Critter picked his cowboy boots and his teddy bear.

"Little Critter, we can put your bicycle on the back of the car, but you won't need your football helmet and skateboard at the farm."

"Okay, Mom. Grandpa and I will have lots to do anyway. We can go fishing, play baseball, ride the horses, and play checkers."

"Little Critter, you will have fun, but don't forget that a farm is a busy place. Grandma and Grandpa have a lot to do every day. Maybe you could help," said Mrs. Critter.

"Yes, I can help!" said Little Critter.

Little Sister popped into the room. "I can help, too! I want to go to the farm, too!"

Mrs. Critter said, "Little Sister, this time it's Little Critter's turn to visit. Next time it will be your turn. You will do fun things here at home."

"But I want my turn now!" said Little Sister.

Mr. Critter called upstairs, "Okay, everyone to bed early tonight. We have a long drive tomorrow!"

Name ______________________

Thinking Skills

Directions: Answer the questions about the story.

1. What is the main idea of the story?

____

____

____

2. What two things did Little Critter pack?

____

____

3. What did Little Sister want to do?

____

____

4. Why did Mrs. Critter say Little Critter would not need his football helmet and skateboard?

____

____

5. What would you pack if you were going to visit a farm?

____

____

____

Reading Skills

Directions: Write a word from the story that means the opposite of each word below.

1. short ____________
2. late ____________
3. front ____________
4. calm ____________
5. later ____________
6. work ____________

Directions: Write the plural of each word below. Remember, *plural* means more than one.

1. horse ____________
2. boot ____________
3. thing ____________
4. farm ____________
5. bag ____________

A Long Drive

Read to find out why it is a long trip.

The next morning, everyone got in the car and buckled their seat belts. Little Sister tried to bring her suitcase, but Mom said, "Next time, Little Sister."

After they were driving a short while, Little Sister said, "I have to go to the bathroom." Mr. Critter stopped at a McCritter's restaurant. Mrs. Critter took Little Sister inside.

The family drove on. Soon there were fewer buildings and houses, and more green fields. "Farm country is beautiful, isn't it?" said Mrs. Critter.

Little Sister tapped Mom on the shoulder. "Mom, I have to go again."

"Okay, Honey, we'll stop as soon as we can."

This time, Mr. Critter stopped at a gas station. Mrs. Critter took Little Sister inside. "Dad, we're never going to get there!" said Little Critter.

"Sure, we will. We'll be there in no time," said Mr. Critter cheerfully. The Critters continued their trip. It was not long until Mrs. Critter felt another tap on her shoulder. It wasn't Little Sister this time.

"Okay, Little Critter, we'll stop as soon as we can," she said.

Name ______________________________

Thinking Skills

Directions: Answer the questions about the story.

1. What is the main idea of the story?

____

____

____

____

2. What did Little Sister try to do?

____

____

3. What two stops did Mr. Critter make?

____

____

4. Describe what the Critter family saw on their drive.

____

____

5. Why was Little Critter upset?

____

____

Reading Skills

Directions: Write each group of words from the story in **ABC** order.

1. morning ______________
   stop ______________
   gas ______________
   can ______________

2. farm ______________
   soon ______________
   took ______________
   houses ______________

Language Skills

Directions: Circle the verb that best completes each sentence about the story. Then, write the verb in the blank.

1. Little Critter ______________ his seat belt.

   buckling buckled buckle

2. Little Critter had to ______________ to the bathroom.

   gone went go

3. Little Critter ______________ Mom's shoulder.

   tap tapped tapping

4. Dad ______________ the car to the farm.

   drive driven drove

Cleaning Up

Let's see how Little Critter helps out after lunch.

After a long drive, the Critters were very glad to be at the farm. Grandma and Grandpa were waiting on the front porch. They had a big lunch ready for the family. The Critters ate chicken soup and grilled cheese sandwiches, drank pink lemonade, and enjoyed cake for dessert.

"Grandma, I can help clean up!" said Little Critter. "I will wash the dishes."

"Why, that would be very nice of you, Little Critter," said Grandma.

Little Critter cleared the dirty dishes from the table. He only dropped one plate, one fork, and half a grilled cheese sandwich. He piled the dishes in the sink and ran warm water over them. Little Critter added some soap. Soon, there were soap bubbles flowing from the sink to the floor. Little Critter was very wet.

"I'm so glad I could help, Grandma!" said Little Critter, as he wiped some bubbles off his nose.

"I am too, Little Critter," replied Grandma. "But, we don't want you to do all the work by yourself!" Grandma and Mr. Critter decided they would help out, too.

Name ______________________

Thinking Skills

Directions: Answer the questions about the story.

1. What did the Critter family have for dessert?

____

____

2. What did Little Critter do to help?

____

____

____

3. What flowed from the sink?

____

____

____

4. How do you think Little Critter felt when he was helping?

____

____

____

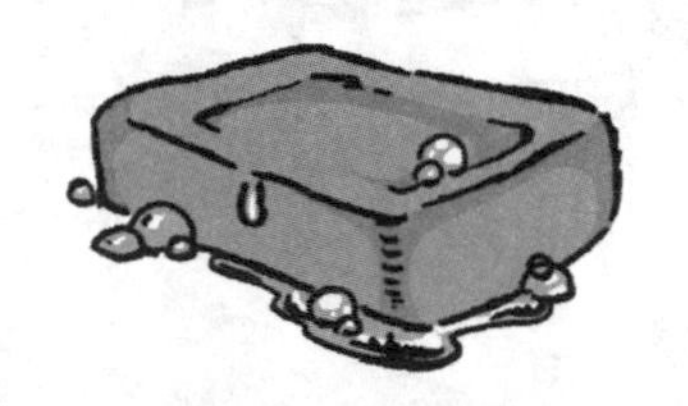

Reading Skills

Directions: Write a word from the story that rhymes with each word below.

1. bunch ____________
2. think ____________
3. wishes ____________
4. growing ____________
5. able ____________

Directions: Write two sentences that describe how you help out at home.

1. ______________________

____

____

2. ______________________

____

____

Language Skills

Directions: Write the past tense of each verb below.

1. clear ____________
2. eat ____________
3. drink ____________
4. wipe ____________
5. drop ____________

Saying Good-bye

How does Little Critter feel when Mom and Dad leave?

Soon it was time for Mr. and Mrs. Critter and Little Sister to go home. Little Critter hugged his parents and his sister good-bye.

He said, "Are you sure you have to leave now? Maybe you should all stay for the week, too!"

Mr. Critter said, "Little Critter, this is your special visit. Just you and Grandma and Grandpa. You will have lots of fun."

"Maybe I should go with you. Who is going to help Little Sister with her coloring books?" asked Little Critter.

"We will help her, Little Critter," answered Mrs. Critter.

"Oh, no! I think I forgot my pajamas," said Little Critter.

"Honey, I packed those for you," said Mrs. Critter. "You will be fine."

Just then Grandpa came out with his checkers set. Grandpa had made the set himself. He had painted the checkers to look like chocolate and vanilla cookies.

"Little Critter, how about a game of checkers?" asked Grandpa.

"Oh, boy! Checkers! I love these checkers!" said Little Critter, as he ran into Grandpa. Checkers flew everywhere. "Bye, Mom! Bye, Dad! Bye, Little Sister!"

"Good-bye, Little Critter. We'll see you soon."

Name ____________________

Thinking Skills

Directions: Answer the questions about the story.

1. What is the main idea of the story?

____

2. How do you think Little Critter was feeling in the story?

____

3. What did Little Critter think that he forgot?

____

4. What did Grandpa bring outside?

____

Reading Skills

Directions: Write a sentence that describes the picture below.

____

Directions: Number the sentences **1**, **2**, **3**, and **4** to show what happened first, second, third, and last.

_____ Mom, Dad, and Little Sister said "Goodbye, Little Critter."

_____ It was time for Mr. and Mrs. Critter and Little Sister to go home.

_____ Little Critter thought he forgot to pack his pajamas.

_____ Grandpa brought his checkers set outside.

Directions: Write the root word for each word below.

1. painted _______________
2. hugged _______________
3. coloring _______________
4. cookies _______________
5. going _______________

Taking Care of the Goats

Read to find out what Little Critter feeds to the goats.

After they said good-bye, Grandpa and Little Critter got to work.

"First, we'll take care of the goats," said Grandpa.

"Are we going to feed them tin cans?" asked Little Critter. "I read a story at school about a goat that ate garbage."

"Well, Little Critter, goats can't really eat metal. They might like to chew the paper off of a can, though. They'll try to eat just about anything," said Grandpa.

Just then, the mother goat tried to munch on Little Critter's pants.

"Hey!" cried Little Critter. He tugged his leg away from the goat. Then, a baby goat started eating Little Critter's shirt.

"Let's get these goats some food quick!" said Grandpa.

Grandpa showed Little Critter the feed for the goats. It was a mix of hay and corn and a few vegetables. The baby goats ate right out of Little Critter's hand. Then they chased each other and jumped around the pen.

"Baby goats are funny!" said Little Critter.

"Baby goats are called *kids*," said Grandpa. "And the mother goat is called a *nanny*."

Name ____________________

Thinking Skills

Directions: Answer the questions about the story.

1. What is the main idea of the story?

____

____

____

2. What did Little Critter think he should feed the goats?

____

____

3. Why did Little Critter think the baby goats were funny?

____

____

4. What did the goats try to eat?

____

____

Reading Skills

Directions: Number the sentences **1**, **2**, **3**, and **4** to show what happened first, second, third, and last in the story.

_____ Grandpa said they would take care of the goats.

_____ A baby goat started to eat Little Critter's shirt.

_____ Little Critter's parents said good-bye.

_____ Little Critter thought that the goats would eat tin cans.

Language Skills

Directions: Write four sentences. Use one word from below in each sentence.

paper	pants
goats	chased

1. ________________________________

____

2. ________________________________

____

3. ________________________________

____

4. ________________________________

____

Bedtime

Read to see what helps Little Critter fall asleep.

Later that evening, Grandma showed Little Critter his room. "I get to sleep in that big bed?" asked Little Critter.

"Yes, it's all yours," said Grandma.

Little Critter climbed into the bed. Grandma tucked him under the quilt. "This bed is much bigger than my bed at home," he said.

"Good-night, Little Critter," said Grandma.

"Good-night, Grandma," replied Little Critter.

Grandma turned off the light. The room was much darker than Little Critter's room at home.

"Grandma, I can't sleep. It's too dark," said Little Critter.

Grandma said, "Well, I'll turn on this night light for you, dear." Little Critter closed his eyes.

"Grandma, I still can't sleep," said Little Critter.

Grandma came into the room and turned on the light. "I know what's missing," she said. Grandma gave Little Critter his teddy bear. Little Critter hugged his bear as Grandma left the room again.

"I STILL can't sleep," called Little Critter.

This time Grandpa answered, "I know what will help, Little Critter. Come into the hallway."

Grandpa handed the telephone to Little Critter. "Hello?" he said, smiling. "Good-night, Mom." Little Critter was soon fast asleep.

Name ____________________

Thinking Skills

Directions: Answer the questions about the story.

1. Why did Little Critter have trouble sleeping?

____

____

____

2. What did Grandma do to make Little Critter feel better?

____

____

3. What did Grandma give to Little Critter?

____

____

4. What did Grandpa do to help?

____

____

____

Reading Skills

Directions: Circle the word that best completes each sentence about the story. Then, write the word in the blank.

1. This bed is much __________ than my bed at home.

   smaller bigger nicer

2. Little Critter __________ his bear.

   lost threw hugged

3. Little Critter __________ into the bed.

   fell crawled climbed

4. Grandpa __________ the telephone to Little Critter.

   sent handed ended

5. The room was much __________ than Little Critter's room at home.

   darker older louder

Directions: Write a word from the story that rhymes with each word below.

1. boom __________
2. moon __________
3. such __________
4. burned __________
5. creep __________
6. light __________

Early Morning

Read to see when the farm day begins.

Little Critter woke up to the sound of dishes clinking in the kitchen. He went into the bathroom. He washed his face, combed his fur, and brushed both of his teeth. He put on some clean clothes. His Critter watch said 7:00. Time for breakfast!

"Little Critter, I'll be in town most of the day, so you'll have to take care of Grandpa," said Grandma.

"Okay, Grandma," said Little Critter.

"Help yourself to breakfast, and I'll see you later," she said.

Little Critter ate a bowl of cereal and drank some juice. *I know,* he thought, *I'll make Grandpa some breakfast and bring it upstairs to him!*

Little Critter found a tray. He put some cereal, some milk, and some juice on the tray for Grandpa. Little Critter wobbled upstairs with the tray. But when he got there, the bed was made with no Grandpa in it.

As Little Critter was coming back downstairs, Grandpa walked in the kitchen door.

"Grandpa, I made you some breakfast!" said Little Critter.

"Well thanks, Little Critter, but I had breakfast two hours ago. You see, farm work starts very early around here!"

Name ______________________

Thinking Skills

Directions: Answer the questions about the story.

1. What did Little Critter make Grandpa for breakfast?

____

____

2. Where was Grandma going?

____

____

3. What time did Grandpa wake up? How do you know?

____

____

____

____

4. Why do you think that Grandpa gets up so early?

____

____

____

____

Reading Skills

Directions: Write each group of words from the story in **ABC** order.

1. woke ______
   went ______
   watch ______
   was ______
2. breakfast ______
   bowl ______
   bathroom ______
   bed ______

Directions: Write a sentence that describes your favorite breakfast.

____

____

Language Skills

Directions: Use the list of words below to make three compound words. Then, write three other compound words that you know.

break	up	bath
stairs	room	fast

1. ______________________
2. ______________________
3. ______________________

1. ______________________
2. ______________________
3. ______________________

The Pigpen

Read to find out how Little Critter helps with the pigs.

"Okay, Little Critter, let's feed the pigs," said Grandpa. Little Critter followed his grandfather to the pigpen. The pigs were rolling around in the mud. Little Critter held his nose. He looked around the pen. He saw one enormous mother pig, and he counted twelve squealing piglets.

"Wow, Grandpa, that's a lot of baby pigs," said Little Critter, as he petted the soft, velvety hair of a piglet.

"Pigs have more babies than any other animal on the farm," said Grandpa. "And they're very smart animals."

Little Critter and Grandpa filled the pig troughs with slop. Grandpa said slop was made of all the scraps from the kitchen, like potato peels and apple cores. The heavy buckets of slop were almost as big as Little Critter. Little Critter and Grandpa gave the pigs water to drink and sprayed the ground with more water.

"Those pigs love to play in the mud as much as I do," said Little Critter.

"They sure do. It helps keep the bugs off. Pigs stay cool by laying in the mud and the puddles," said Grandpa. "But, I think I know a better way for us to get cool."

Name ______________________________

Thinking Skills

Directions: Answer the questions about the story.

1. What is the pig slop made of?

____

____

2. List two things that Grandpa taught Little Critter about pigs.

____

____

____

____

3. What else did Grandpa and Little Critter do for the pigs besides feed them?

____

____

4. What do you think Grandpa and Little Critter will do next?

____

____

Reading Skills

Directions: Write three sentences that describe the picture on page 90.

1. ______________________________

____

2. ______________________________

____

3. ______________________________

____

Directions: Write a word from the story that means the opposite of each word below.

1. tiny ______________
2. on ______________
3. hard ______________
4. warm ______________
5. light ______________

Language Skills

Directions: Write a contraction from the story that stands for each pair of words.

1. they are ______________
2. let us ______________
3. that is ______________

Cooling Off

Read to see how Grandpa and Little Critter cool off.

After feeding the pigs, the chickens, and the turkeys, Little Critter and Grandpa put on their swimsuits.

"A little dip in the water will cool us off," said Grandpa. They walked down the hill to the pond. They put their towels down on the grass. Butterflies floated around the pond, and crickets chirped. The sun sparkled on the water.

Little Critter stuck his toe in the pond. A frog leaped over his foot. Little Critter jumped back. He looked down and saw tiny fish swimming around.

"You go in first, Grandpa," said Little Critter.

"Oh, frogs and fish won't hurt you, Little Critter," said Grandpa. "Maybe one day this week we can come down here and do some fishing."

"That would be great! I love fishing!" said Little Critter.

Grandpa jumped in the water and swam around. Little Critter paddled around after him. The cool water felt wonderful on such a hot, sticky day. They swam for just a few minutes.

"Well, Little Critter, I'm afraid that's all the time we have. Let's dry off, eat some lunch, and get back to work."

Name ______________________________

Thinking Skills

Directions: Answer the questions about the story.

1. What time of year do you think the story takes place? Why?

____

____

2. What were Grandpa and Little Critter going to do after their swim?

____

____

3. Would you like to swim in Grandpa's pond? Why or why not?

____

____

Reading Skills

Directions: Write a word from the story that has the same beginning blend as each word below.

1. fly ____________
2. fry ____________
3. grow ____________
4. swan ____________
5. step ____________

Directions: Write a sentence that describes the picture on this page.

____

____

____

Language Skills

Directions: Write the past tense of each verb below.

1. float ____________
2. jump ____________
3. swim ____________
4. paddle ____________
5. walk ____________

Sandwiches for Grandpa

Read to see what Little Critter makes for lunch.

"Grandpa, since you didn't get to eat the breakfast I made you, maybe I can make you some lunch," said Little Critter.

"That's a fine idea, Little Critter," said Grandpa.

Little Critter went into the kitchen. He thought he would make his favorite kind of sandwiches for Grandpa.

First, Little Critter looked for the things he would need. He got orange juice and pickles out of the refrigerator. He found bread in the breadbox. He found some peanut butter and potato chips in the cupboard.

This will be a delicious lunch, and I'm helping like Mom said, he thought. *I can do this all by myself!*

Grandpa was waiting for him out on the front porch. Little Critter came out with two sandwiches and two glasses of milk.

"What did you make for us, Little Critter?" asked Grandpa.

"I made my famous peanut butter and pickle sandwiches with orange juice and potato chips!" he said. "Yum!"

"Yum-yum," said Grandpa. Then he took a small bite. He chewed very slowly.

"It's fun to be here with you, Grandpa," said Little Critter.

"It's fun to be with you too, Little Critter," said Grandpa.

Name ____________________

Thinking Skills

Directions: Answer the questions about the story.

1. What is the main idea of the story?

2. What did Little Critter make for lunch?

3. How did Little Critter feel about making lunch for Grandpa?

4. Do you think Grandpa liked the lunch? Why or why not?

Reading Skills

Directions: Write two words from the story that have each vowel sound.

1. Long e
2. Short i
3. Short u
4. Long i
5. Short e
6. Long a

Language Skills

Directions: Write three sentences. Use one word from below in each sentence.

famous	delicious	favorite

1.
2.
3.

Milking the Cows

Read to see what Little Critter learns about cows.

"Little Critter, it's time to milk the cows again," said Grandpa.

"Why do you have to milk them again?" asked Little Critter.

"When a cow has a calf she makes milk for the baby. She makes so much extra milk that we must milk her twice a day," Grandpa said.

Grandpa sat down on a stool and began to milk a cow named Jody. "On big farms, they have milking machines to do the work," said Grandpa. "Since we only have three cows at our little farm, Grandma and I can milk them."

Little Critter watched the milk stream into the bucket. Jody was very calm. Little Critter petted her smooth, brown coat as Grandpa milked. Little Critter fed her bunches of hay. "Boy, does she eat a lot!" he said.

"That's because cows have four stomachs," said Grandpa.

"Four stomachs! No wonder she eats so much!" said Little Critter.

"She makes milk from eating hay, grass, and grain," said Grandpa. "Milk is used to make things like cheese, butter, and yogurt."

"And ice cream!" said Little Critter. "Thanks for the ice cream, Jody!"

Name ______________________________

Thinking Skills

Directions: Answer the questions about the story.

1. What is the main idea of the story?

____

____

____

2. What did Little Critter do while Grandpa milked Jody?

____

____

3. What kinds of foods are made from milk?

____

____

4. How does a big farm do things differently?

____

____

____

Reading Skills

Directions: Write **F** next to the statements that are **facts** and **O** next to the statements that are **opinions**.

_____ 1. Cows have four stomachs.

_____ 2. Cows are the smartest animals in the world.

_____ 3. Cheese and yogurt can be made from milk.

_____ 4. Ice cream is the best snack.

_____ 5. Cows feed milk to their calves.

_____ 6. A mother cow makes extra milk.

Directions: Write three sentences that describe the picture on page 96.

1. ______________________________

____

2. ______________________________

____

3. ______________________________

____

Picking Berries

Read to see if Little Critter likes blackberries.

The next morning, Grandpa went to town to buy farm supplies. Grandma woke Little Critter up early to help feed all the animals.

"Little Critter," said Grandma, "we have something really fun to do next." Grandma took two plastic bowls out of the cupboard. She handed one to Little Critter.

"What are we going to do with these bowls?" asked Little Critter.

"We're going to fill them with berries," said Grandma.

"Berries! Yum!" said Little Critter.

Little Critter and Grandma walked out to the blackberry patch behind the barn. The branches were filled with large, dark, purple berries.

"Pick the really dark ones," said Grandma. "Those are the sweetest!"

"Okay," said Little Critter as he picked a berry and ate it. A wonderful sweet flavor filled his mouth. "Mmmmm, these are so good."

"We need to fill these bowls so we can make pies for the Critter Country Fair tomorrow. We are going to enter the pie contest," said Grandma.

"Oh, boy, a pie contest! I can't wait," said Little Critter.

Little Critter started picking berries, but he couldn't resist tasting them. After a while, Grandma's bowl was almost full.

"How are you doing, Little Critter?" asked Grandma. She looked at his bowl. "I think there are more berries in your belly than in your bowl!"

Name ______________________________

Thinking Skills

Directions: Answer the questions about the story.

1. What is the main idea of the story?

   ____

   ____

   ____

2. Where does this story take place?

   ____

   ____

3. Why did Grandma tell Little Critter to pick the dark berries?

   ____

   ____

4. Why were Grandma and Little Critter picking berries?

   ____

   ____

5. What do you think will happen next?

   ____

   ____

   ____

Reading Skills

Directions: Write two sentences that tell about the picture below.

1. ______________________________

   ____

2. ______________________________

   ____

Language Skills

Directions: Write an adjective to describe each word below.

1. ____________ berries
2. ____________ bowl
3. ____________ pies
4. ____________ belly

Baking Pies

Read about the two bakers.

Grandma and Little Critter washed the blackberries in the kitchen sink. They mixed the berries with sugar to fill the pie. Grandma got out the flour and shortening to make dough for the crust.

"Little Critter, we need to roll out this dough to make the crust," said Grandma.

Grandma showed Little Critter how to roll out the dough smooth and flat. They put one half of the dough in the bottom of the pie plate. Then Grandma let Little Critter pour in the berries.

"Grandma, this is going to be the best pie at the Critter Country Fair!" said Little Critter.

"I don't know about that, Little Critter. There are going to be a lot of delicious pies in the contest," said Grandma.

They put the other piece of dough over the top of the berries. Grandma showed Little Critter how to squeeze the edges of the dough together so the berries wouldn't leak out. Little Critter made the extra dough into heart shapes to decorate the top.

After that, Grandma and Little Critter made two more pies.

"Good work, Little Critter! I will put the last pie in the oven," said Grandma.

Name ____________________

Thinking Skills

Directions: Answer the questions about the story.

1. What is the main idea of the story?

____

____

____

2. What was the first thing that Grandma and Little Critter did?

____

____

3. What was the last thing Grandma and Little Critter did?

____

____

4. What did Little Critter do with the extra dough?

____

____

____

Reading Skills

Directions: Number the sentences **1**, **2**, **3**, and **4** to show what happened first, second, third, and last in the story.

_____ They rolled out the pie dough.

_____ They put the other piece of dough over the berries.

_____ Grandma and Little Critter made two more pies.

_____ Grandma and Little Critter mixed the berries with sugar.

Directions: Write each group of words from the story in **ABC** order.

1. flour ______________
   fill ______________
   for ______________
   flat ______________

2. put ______________
   plate ______________
   pour ______________
   pie ______________

Picking Vegetables

Read to find out what the Critters will have for dinner.

When the pies were done, Grandma and Little Critter headed out to the vegetable garden with a big basket.

"Let's pick some potatoes for dinner tonight," said Grandma.

Little Critter looked around. "I don't see any potatoes," he said.

"Potatoes are a root vegetable. They grow underground, just like carrots and beets," said Grandma. Together, Little Critter and Grandma dug up some potatoes and some carrots.

Grandma said, "The green tomatoes aren't quite ready to eat yet. Pick some nice, ripe, red ones. Did you know every flower on that tomato plant will become a tomato? It's like magic, isn't it, Little Critter?"

"A flower turning into a tomato is magic!" said Little Critter, as he pulled the bright tomatoes off the plants.

Little Critter and his grandma added lettuce, green beans, and purple beets to their basket. Little Critter thought, **I'LL BET THOSE PURPLE BEETS TASTE SWEET LIKE THE BLACKBERRIES! YUM.**

"Grandma, don't you have any pumpkins growing? We can make pumpkin pies next!"

Grandma sighed. "Oh, my! Pumpkins won't be ready until fall, Little Critter," she said. "Besides, we've got an awful lot of blackberry pie to eat first!"

Name ____________________

Thinking Skills

Directions: Answer the questions about the story.

1. What is the main idea of the story?

2. Where does the story take place?

3. What color are tomatoes that are ready to eat?

4. How are carrots and potatoes alike? How are they different?

5. Why don't Little Critter and Grandma pick pumpkins?

Reading Skills

Directions: Write a sentence that describes the picture below.

Directions: Write four sentences. Use one word from below in each sentence.

lettuce	underground
magic	sweet

1.

2.

3.

4.

Veggies for Dinner

Read to find out if Little Critter likes a new vegetable.

"Please pass the potatoes," said Little Critter.

"Why, you have such nice manners, Little Critter," said Grandpa.

"Mom always likes us to use our good manners," said Little Critter. "Did you have a good day, Grandpa?"

"I had a very good day in town," said Grandpa. "I got some new tools, some feed, and I bought a few new hens."

"I helped Grandma today," said Little Critter.

"You sure did," answered Grandma. "I'm just surprised you don't have a tummy ache from eating all those blackberries."

"Please pass the beets," said Little Critter.

"Oh, these fresh beets are delicious!" said Grandma.

Little Critter was ready for a wonderful, sweet bite. But, when he tasted the beets, they were not sweet. They were sour. They did not taste good. Little Critter remembered his manners. He chewed very slowly and swallowed.

"I thought these would taste like berries," said Little Critter with a frown.

Grandma and Grandpa smiled at each other. "I didn't like beets either when I was your age," said Grandpa. "I have an after-dinner treat for you that might be better." Grandpa got up and handed Little Critter a purple stick of candy.

"Oh!" exclaimed Little Critter. "This will taste much better than beets!"

Name ______________________________

Thinking Skills

Directions: Answer the questions about the story.

1. What is the main idea of the story?

____

____

____

2. What did Grandpa buy in town?

____

____

____

3. What did the beets taste like?

____

____

____

4. What did Little Critter expect the beets to taste like?

____

____

5. What did Grandpa bring for Little Critter?

____

____

Reading Skills

Directions: Write a sentence that describes the picture below.

____

____

____

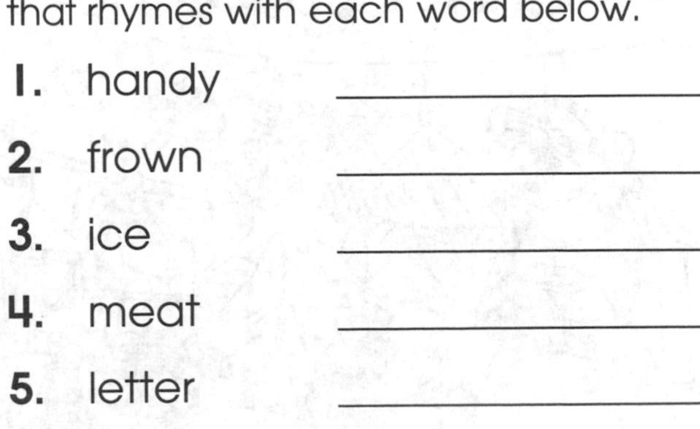

Directions: Write a word from the story that rhymes with each word below.

1. handy ____________
2. frown ____________
3. ice ____________
4. meat ____________
5. letter ____________
6. such ____________

The Critter Country Fair

Read to see what is going on at the fair.

It was a hot, bright summer morning. Little Critter and his grandparents headed for the Critter Country Fair.

When they arrived, Little Critter looked all around. The rides whirled. The animals **MOOED** and **CROWED** and **BAAED** in the barns. Music played loudly. Fair workers called out to come play their games. There were contests to show off garden vegetables, fresh-baked pies, and homemade jars of jelly. The warm air smelled of sweet cotton candy and spicy mustard.

Grandma needed to bring their pie to the cooking tent. The pie would be kept in a cool place until it was time for the contest.

"What should we do, Little Critter?" asked Grandpa, as he wiped his brow.

"Let's play a game, Grandpa!" said Little Critter. "Let's play that game where you spray water in the clown's mouth and blow up a balloon."

Little Critter and Grandpa sat down at the game. Little Critter held his sprayer tightly and aimed at the clown's mouth. He turned to talk to Grandpa when suddenly the game began! Little Critter sprayed water all over Grandpa's shirt instead of in the clown's mouth.

"Well, Little Critter, that's one way to cool off!" said Grandpa.

Name ____________________

Thinking Skills

Directions: Answer the questions about the story.

1. What is the main idea of the story?

___

___

___

2. Describe three things that were happening at the Critter Country Fair.

___

___

___

3. What kind of game did Little Critter and Grandpa play?

___

___

4. How did Grandpa cool off?

___

___

___

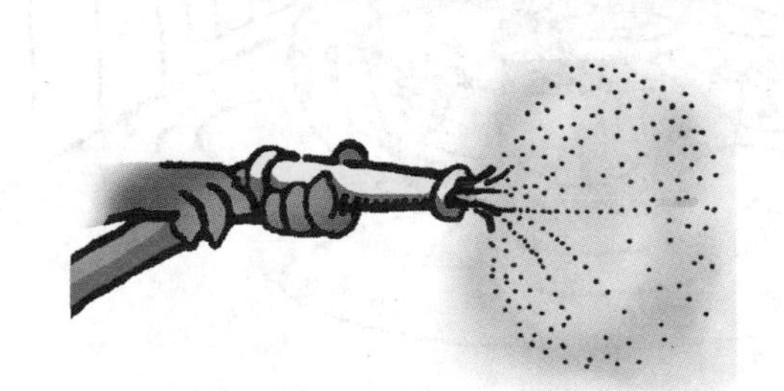

Reading Skills

Directions: Circle the verb that best completes each sentence. Then, write the word in the blank.

1. Fair workers called out to come ________ their games.

   place play please

2. The air ________ of cotton candy.

   sang smiled smelled

3. Little Critter ________ Grandpa's shirt.

   sprayed sprang spring

4. Music ________ loudly.

   sprayed played paid

Directions: Write an adjective to describe each word below.

1. ____________ game
2. ____________ clown
3. ____________ vegetables
4. ____________ shirt
5. ____________ contest

The Twisty Teacup

Read to see if the Twisty Teacup is a fun ride.

"Grandpa, let's go on a ride now!" said Little Critter.

"Which ride would you like to go on?" asked Grandpa. "How about the merry-go-round?"

"The merry-go-round is for critters littler than me. I want to go on the Twisty Teacup ride!" said Little Critter.

"Okay, Little Critter. That ride spins an awful lot. I will stay here and watch you," said Grandpa.

Little Critter got in line with the other critters. He gave the fair worker his ticket. As Little Critter sat in a teacup, another fair worker fastened his safety belt. He held on tightly. The ride began slowly. **THIS IS NOTHING**, Little Critter thought to himself. **I WON'T GET DIZZY.**

Just then the ride sped up. The teacup whirled Little Critter around in circles. The kids around him squealed.

"Whoooaaaa!" screamed Little Critter. He closed his eyes, but that made him feel more dizzy.

Little Critter was very happy when the ride was over. Everything was still spinning when he stumbled out of the teacup.

"You look a little pale. Are you okay, Little Critter?" asked Grandpa.

Little Critter wobbled. "I think so Grandpa, but maybe we should go on the merry-go-round next time!" said Little Critter.

Name ____________________

Thinking Skills

Directions: Answer the questions about the story.

1. Which ride did Little Critter want to try?

____

____

2. What did Grandpa tell Little Critter about that ride?

____

____

3. How did Little Critter feel about the merry-go-round at the beginning of the story? How did he feel about it at the end of the story?

____

____

____

____

4. What do you think Little Critter and Grandpa will do next?

____

____

Reading Skills

Directions: Number the sentences **1**, **2**, **3**, and **4** to show what happened first, second, third, and last in the story.

____ Grandpa asked Little Critter if he was okay.

____ Little Critter did not want to ride the merry-go-round.

____ The fair worker fastened Little Critter's safety belt.

____ Little Critter was happy when the ride was over.

Directions: In your own words, write the meaning of each word below. Then use one of the words in a sentence.

1. pale ______________________

____

____

2. wobbled ______________________

____

____

3. dizzy ______________________

____

____

Two Pie Contests

Read to see why Little Critter isn't hungry for pie.

Little Critter, Grandma, and Grandpa entered the cooking tent just as the pie contest began. The judges were tasting each pie and making notes. Little Critter's stomach growled. He saw a sign in the next tent for a different kind of pie contest.

"Grandma, can I go watch the pie-eating contest?" asked Little Critter.

"Sure," said Grandma. "Then come back here afterwards."

When Little Critter walked into the tent, someone announced, "The pie-eating contest will now begin. All contestants to the front table, please."

The smell of pie made Little Critter's stomach growl even more. He sat down at the table. Someone placed a blueberry pie in front of him.

"On your mark, get set, go!" Little Critter was busy looking for his fork while the other contestants stuck their faces in their pies! Little Critter did the same. He ate and ate, but he could not finish. The winner had eaten five pies!

Little Critter rubbed his tummy. He tried to wipe the sticky berries off his fur and his clothes. He dragged himself back to the cooking tent. Grandma was holding a piece of the pie she and Little Critter had made. It had a red ribbon on it.

"We took second place, Little Critter!" said Grandma. "Look! I saved you a nice, big piece!"

Name ____________________

Thinking Skills

Directions: Answer the questions about the story.

1. What were the judges in the cooking tent doing?

2. What contest did Little Critter join?

3. How many pies did the winner eat?

4. How do you think Little Critter felt at the end of the story?

5. Do you think Little Critter will eat the piece of pie Grandma saved for him? Why or why not?

Reading Skills

Directions: Write each group of words from the story in **ABC** order.

1. sign
   stomach
   saved
   someone

2. tent
   tasting
   their
   table

3. pie
   please
   placed
   piece

4. five
   fur
   faces
   finish

Directions: Write a sentence that describes the picture below.

A Letter From Mom and Dad

Read to see what Mr. and Mrs. Critter write.

When Grandma, Grandpa, and Little Critter got home from the country fair, they found a letter for Little Critter in the mailbox. Little Critter read it out loud to his grandparents.

DEAR LITTLE CRITTER,

WE ARE GLAD THAT YOU ARE HAVING FUN AT THE FARM. IT SOUNDS LIKE YOU ARE LEARNING A LOT ABOUT FARM LIFE. WHICH ANIMALS ARE YOUR FAVORITES?

YESTERDAY, WE TOOK LITTLE SISTER TO THE ZOO. SHE LIKED THE ELEPHANTS THE BEST. AFTER THE ZOO, WE ALL GOT SOME ICE CREAM. THE WEATHER HAS BEEN VERY WARM. NO WONDER YOU AND GRANDPA JUMPED IN THE POND!

YOU ARE A BIG HELP TO YOUR GRANDPARENTS. GRANDMA AND GRANDPA ARE HAPPY TO HAVE YOU THERE.

WE MISS YOU A LOT. BUT, WE'LL SEE YOU IN JUST A COUPLE OF DAYS. YOU CAN TELL US MORE ABOUT YOUR VISIT!

LOVE,

MOM AND DAD

P.S. LITTLE SISTER MISSES YOU A LOT, TOO!

Grandpa said, "We sure are glad to have you, Little Critter. We will miss you when you go home."

Little Critter said, "I like being here, too. Just me and my

Name ____________________

Thinking Skills

Directions: Answer the questions about the story.

1. What did Mom and Dad write in their letter to Little Critter?

____

____

____

2. How do you think Little Critter will feel when it is time to go home?

____

____

3. Write three things that Little Critter could write about to his family.

____

____

____

4. What does a "P.S." mean at the end of a letter?

____

____

____

Reading Skills

Directions: Circle the word that best completes each sentence. Then, write the word in the blank.

1. They __________ a letter in the mailbox.

   bound hound found

2. We are glad that you are __________ fun at the farm.

   being having seeing

3. Little Sister __________ the elephants best.

   licked looked liked

4. We will __________ you in a couple of days.

   saw seeing see

5. The weather has __________ very warm.

   been seen was

Language Skills

Directions: Write two sentences. Use one word from below in each sentence.

found	weather

1. ____________________

____

2. ____________________

____

Stormy Night

Read to find out how Grandpa helps Little Critter.

Little Critter was getting ready for bed when there was a loud crash of thunder. Little Critter dove under the bed and closed his eyes.

Grandpa came into the room. "Are you afraid of the storm?" he asked.

"I hate thunder and lightning," said Little Critter as he came out from under the bed.

"You are safe inside, Little Critter," said Grandpa. "We need rain so our crops will grow."

The thunder boomed again and the lightning flashed. Little Critter covered his face.

"Were you scared of storms when you were little, Grandpa?" asked Little Critter.

"Yes," said Grandpa.

"How come you aren't afraid now?" asked Little Critter.

"One time I watched a thunderstorm with my grandpa. At first, I closed my eyes. Then I found out that if I watched the lightning, I wasn't so scared," said Grandpa.

Little Critter and Grandpa listened to the rain hitting the window. The next time the lightning flashed, Little Critter tried not to close his eyes. He squeezed Grandpa's hand. The lightning lit up the farmyard.

In a little while, the thunder wasn't so loud anymore. The lightning wasn't so bright.

"Grandpa, I think I'm not scared anymore," said Little Critter.

"Good night, Little Critter," said Grandpa. "Call if you need me."

"Good night, Grandpa," said Little Critter.

Name ______________________

Thinking Skills

Directions: Answer the questions about the story.

1. Where does this story take place?

____

____

2. How do you know that Little Critter was afraid of the thunderstorm?

____

____

____

3. How did Grandpa help Little Critter?

____

____

____

4. What do you think Little Critter will do the next time there is a thunderstorm?

____

____

____

Reading Skills

Directions: Number the sentences **1**, **2**, **3**, and **4** to show what happened first, second, third, and last in the story.

_____ Little Critter dove under the bed.

_____ There was a loud crash of thunder.

_____ Little Critter wasn't scared anymore.

_____ Grandpa told Little Critter a story.

Directions: Write a word from the story that rhymes with each word below.

1. mashed ____________

2. race ____________

3. hall ____________

4. main ____________

5. sound ____________

6. seed ____________

7. mow ____________

8. sitting ____________

Riding the Horses

Read to see what Little Critter learns about horses.

The next day, Little Critter and Grandpa took care of the horses. They fed the horses hay, cleaned out their stalls, and brushed their coats.

Little Critter was brushing a horse called Buttercup. "You are such a nice horse," said Little Critter, as he petted her softly.

"Horses like it when you talk to them," said Grandpa. Grandpa was grooming a very big horse named Old Kicker.

Grandpa showed Little Critter how the horses wore horseshoes.

"Does it hurt when they nail those horseshoes onto their hooves?" asked Little Critter.

"No, it doesn't hurt them at all. Horseshoes help protect the horses' hooves," said Grandpa. "Let's take these horses out for some exercise."

Grandpa strapped a leather saddle on each horse. Then he said, "Use the reins to guide your horse. Pull gently on the right rein to turn to the right. Pull on the left rein to steer left. Pull back on both reins and say 'Whoa' to stop the horse," said Grandpa. "I think we are about ready for our ride."

"I want to ride Old Kicker!" said Little Critter.

Old Kicker jumped on his hind legs and whinnied loudly.

"Maybe you should ride Buttercup today, Little Critter!" exclaimed Grandpa.

Name ____________________

Thinking Skills

Directions: Answer the questions about the story.

1. What is the main idea of the story?

____

____

____

2. List three things that Little Critter and Grandpa did for the horses.

____

____

____

3. Why do horses wear horseshoes?

____

____

4. Would you rather ride Old Kicker or Buttercup? Why?

____

____

____

Reading Skills

Directions: Write three sentences. Use one word from below in each sentence.

hooves	exercise	steer

1. ______________________________

____

2. ______________________________

____

3. ______________________________

____

Language Skills

Directions: Write the past tense of each verb below.

1. clean ____________
2. feed ____________
3. brush ____________
4. say ____________
5. pet ____________
6. call ____________
7. name ____________
8. wear ____________

Shearing the Sheep

Read to see who Little Critter plays with.

Next, Little Critter went to see what Grandma was doing in the sheep pen.

"Why are you feeding that baby sheep with a bottle, Grandma?" asked Little Critter.

"Sometimes we have to help the ewes feed their babies," said Grandma.

"Ewes?" asked Little Critter.

"Mother sheep are called **EWES**," said Grandma. "Would you like to take care of this baby? I am going to shear its mother."

"Shear?" asked Little Critter.

"Yes, I am going to shave the wool off this sheep. Then we will sell the wool. Things like sweaters and blankets are made of wool," said Grandma. "Take this bottle of milk. You can finish feeding this lamb."

When Grandma took the ewe into the barn, the little lamb bleated loudly. Little Critter fed the lamb the bottle of milk. The hungry lamb drank it quickly. Little Critter walked around the pen. The lamb followed him, looking for more milk. Little Critter ran to the other side of the pen, and the playful lamb dashed after him. They chased each other back and forth.

When Grandma brought the ewe back to the pen, the little lamb ran straight to its mother.

"I guess our game of tag is over!" said Little Critter.

Name ______________________________

Thinking Skills

Directions: Answer the questions about the story.

1. What is the main idea of the story?

____

____

2. How would you describe the little lamb?

____

____

3. What kinds of things are made from wool?

____

____

____

Reading Skills

Directions: Write each group of words from the story in **ABC** order.

1. lamb ______________
   little ______________
   finish ______________
   feed ______________
2. milk ______________
   more ______________
   mother ______________
   made ______________
3. bottle ______________
   baby ______________
   blankets ______________
   barn ______________

Directions: Write the root word for each word below.

1. quickly ______________
2. feeding ______________
3. playful ______________
4. asked ______________
5. going ______________
6. dashed ______________

A Bicycle Ride

Read to find out what Little Critter sees on his bicycle ride.

"Grandma, do you want to go for a bike ride?" asked Little Critter.

"Honey, I'd like to, but I've got some things to do here," said Grandma.

"Grandpa, how about you?" asked Little Critter.

"I've got some chores to finish up, Little Critter. You may go. Just stay on the paths here in the farmyard," said Grandpa.

Little Critter thought, **IF LITTLE SISTER WERE HERE, SHE WOULD FOLLOW ME ON HER TRICYCLE.**

Little Critter got his bicycle out of the barn. His mom had hung his helmet on the handlebars.

"I can't go anywhere without my helmet!" said Little Critter.

Little Critter rode past the goats, the sheep, Grandma's garden, and the chicken coop. He rode around the back of the horse barn. Up ahead he saw a big rock in the path. Little Critter stopped. It wasn't a rock at all. It was a brown turtle with orange patterns on its back!

Little Critter did not want to scare the turtle back into its shell. He quietly watched the turtle crawl into the grass. **WOW**, thought Little Critter. **THAT WAS A COOL TURTLE. LITTLE SISTER WOULD REALLY HAVE LIKED THAT TURTLE. I WILL HAVE TO TELL HER ABOUT IT.**

Name ______________________

Thinking Skills

Directions: Answer the questions about the story.

1. Why couldn't Grandma or Grandpa go for a bike ride with Little Critter?

____

____

____

2. What did Little Critter see on his bicycle ride?

____

____

____

3. What did Mom put on Little Critter's bicycle?

____

____

4. How do you know that Little Critter missed Little Sister?

____

____

____

Reading Skills

Directions: Number the sentences **1**, **2**, **3**, and **4** to show what happened first, second, third, and last in the story.

_____ Little Critter got his bicycle out of the barn.

_____ Little Critter saw a brown turtle.

_____ Little Critter asked Grandma to go on a bike ride.

_____ Little Critter put on his helmet.

Directions: Write two sentences that describe the picture below.

1. ______________________

____

2. ______________________

____

A Letter From Little Sister

Read to see what Little Sister sends Little Critter.

When Little Critter came back from his bike ride, Grandma was making some sandwiches in the kitchen. "There's a letter here for you, Little Critter," she said.

"I got another letter?" asked Little Critter. The envelope felt heavy. **WHAT COULD IT BE?** he thought. He opened it up and read it out loud.

DEAR LITTLE CRITTER,

MOM IS HELPING ME WRITE A LETTER TO YOU. IT SOUNDS LIKE YOU ARE HAVING FUN ON THE FARM. I WAS PLAYING WITH SOME OF YOUR TOYS, BUT I PUT THEM AWAY WHEN I WAS DONE. I AM SENDING YOU A PICTURE THAT I DREW.

LOVE,

LITTLE SISTER

Grandma said, "It sounds like your little sister misses you, Little Critter."

"I kind of miss her, too," said Little Critter, "except she always follows me around."

"That's because you're her big brother. She looks up to you," said Grandma.

Little Critter opened up the drawing that Little Sister had made. It was a picture of him with Little Sister. She wrote "Little Sister" and "Big Brother" in black next to each drawing.

"Let's hang that up here in the kitchen, so we can all enjoy it," said Grandma.

Name ____________________

Thinking Skills

Directions: Answer the questions about the story.

1. What is the main idea of the story?

____

____

____

2. What was Grandma doing when Little Critter came in?

____

____

3. Describe the picture that Little Sister drew for Little Critter.

____

____

____

4. Where did Grandma hang the picture? Why?

____

____

____

____

Language Skills

Directions: Write an adjective to describe each noun below.

1. __________ picture
2. __________ letter
3. __________ sandwich
4. __________ kitchen
5. __________ crayon
6. __________ sister

Directions: Write three sentences. Use one noun and adjective pair from above in each sentence.

1. _______________

____

2. _______________

____

3. _______________

____

A Picnic for Dinner

Read to find out who would pack a healthier picnic.

"Grandma, are you making peanut butter and pickle sandwiches?" asked Little Critter.

"No, not today, Little Critter. These are chicken sandwiches. I thought we could go on a picnic for dinner tonight," said Grandma.

"A picnic! I love picnics!" said Little Critter.

Grandma and Grandpa and Little Critter walked to the apple orchard. There were rows and rows of trees filled with small green apples.

"Can we eat these apples, Grandma?" asked Little Critter.

"Not yet. They won't be ready until the fall," she said.

Grandpa spread out the picnic blanket. Grandma put the picnic basket on the blanket.

Grandma had packed chicken sandwiches, coleslaw, carrot sticks, strawberries, and some oatmeal cookies for dessert.

"Next time I can pack the picnic for you, Grandma," said Little Critter, "I'll bring brownies, potato chips, popcorn, cupcakes, and some soda pop. Oh, yeah. And some peanut butter and pickle sandwiches."

Grandma and Grandpa grinned at each other.

"Don't you worry, Little Critter. Grandma is always glad to pack the picnic!" said Grandpa. "She has a knack for putting together a balanced meal."

"I sure do!" said Grandma. "Now eat your sandwich, Little Critter."

Name ____________________

Thinking Skills

Directions: Answer the questions about the story.

1. What is the main idea of the story?

____

____

____

2. What did Grandma pack for the picnic?

____

____

3. What would Little Critter pack?

____

____

4. Whose food is healthier? Why?

____

____

____

Reading Skills

Directions: Write three sentences. Use one word from below in each sentence.

basket	orchard	picnic

1. ______________________________

____

2. ______________________________

____

3. ______________________________

____

Language Skills

Directions: Write a period or question mark at the end of each sentence below.

1. Can we eat these apples _____
2. These are chicken sandwiches _____
3. Next time, I can pack the picnic _____
4. Are you making peanut butter and pickle sandwiches _____
5. Grandma put the picnic basket on the blanket _____

Making a Scarecrow

Read to find out how Grandpa and Little Critter make a scarecrow.

After the picnic, Grandpa and Little Critter walked out to the cornfield. The cornstalks were taller than both of them. There were some large, black birds in the field eating the corn.

"Little Critter, I think we need to make a scarecrow," said Grandpa, "before these crows eat all of our corn."

"A scarecrow! That will be fun to make," said Little Critter.

Grandpa gathered some hay. Little Critter asked Grandma for some old clothes. They made the scarecrow's head by stuffing an old rag with hay and tying the bottom with some rope. Little Critter drew a face with a smile. They stuffed the rest of the clothes with hay and tied them together. They gave the scarecrow one of Grandpa's old fishing hats. Then they tied the scarecrow to a wooden pole.

"How does the scarecrow work, Grandpa?" asked Little Critter.

"We stand it up in the cornfield, Little Critter," said Grandpa. "Hopefully the crows will think it's a real critter and be too scared to come down."

"Watch out, crows! This is the meanest, scariest scarecrow ever!" said Little Critter.

Name ______________________________

Thinking Skills

Directions: Answer the questions about the story.

1. Why did Grandpa think they needed to make a scarecrow?

____

____

2. What did Grandpa and Little Critter use to make the scarecrow?

____

____

____

____

3. What did Little Critter think of the scarecrow?

____

____

____

Reading Skills

Directions: Number the sentences **1**, **2**, **3**, and **4** to show what happened first, second, third, and last in the story.

_____ Grandpa and Little Critter put the scarecrow in the cornfield.

_____ Black birds were in the field eating corn.

_____ Little Critter told the crows to watch out.

_____ Grandpa and Little Critter decided to make a scarecrow.

Directions: Write a word from the story that rhymes with each word below.

1. day ______________
2. knows ______________
3. wink ______________
4. while ______________
5. rack ______________
6. horn ______________
7. feed ______________
8. hole ______________

Fishing at the Pond

Read to see if Little Critter and Grandpa catch any fish.

"Can we go fishing now, Grandpa?" asked Little Critter.

"Yes, we can, Little Critter. All the chores are done for the day!" said Grandpa.

Grandpa and Little Critter headed for the pond with their fishing poles. They sat together on the creaky wooden dock. Crickets chirped and frogs croaked. Bright green dragonflies darted across the water. Grandpa showed Little Critter how to put a worm on the fishhook.

"Be careful," said Grandpa, "the hook is sharp. Now, cast your line, like this." Grandpa flicked his fishing line into the middle of the pond.

When Little Critter tried, his line got caught on Grandpa's hat.

"Sorry, Grandpa," said Little Critter, as he reeled in the soggy hat.

"Try again, Little Critter," said Grandpa.

Little Critter cast his line into the pond again. "I know I'm going to catch the biggest fish in the pond," said Little Critter.

Hours later, Little Critter and Grandpa still had not caught anything. "Fishing takes some patience, doesn't it, Little Critter?" asked Grandpa.

"It sure does, but I think it's fun being here at the pond with you, Grandpa," said Little Critter.

Name ____________________

Thinking Skills

Directions: Answer the questions about the story.

1. Where does this story take place?

____

____

2. What kinds of animals live around the pond?

____

____

____

3. What happened to Little Critter's fishing line?

____

____

4. Do you think Grandpa and Little Critter will catch any fish? Why or why not?

____

____

____

Reading Skills

Directions: Number the sentences **1**, **2**, **3**, and **4** to show what happened first, second, third, and last in the story.

_____ Grandpa showed Little Critter how to put a worm on a fishhook.

_____ Grandpa told Little Critter that it takes patience to fish.

_____ Grandpa and Little Critter decided to go fishing.

_____ Little Critter's line got caught on Grandpa's hat.

Directions: Write two sentences that describe the picture below.

1. ________________________________

____

2. ________________________________

____

Four Shiny Marbles

Read to find out what Little Critter can buy with a dollar.

"Little Critter, would you like to go into town today?" asked Grandpa.

"Sure, Grandpa!" said Little Critter.

Grandma gave Little Critter four shiny quarters. "Buy a treat, Little Critter," said Grandma.

"Thank you, Grandma!" said Little Critter. He put the quarters in his pocket.

In town, Grandpa said, "Let's go into the general store."

"What's the general store?" asked Little Critter.

"It's a place where you can buy anything and everything!" said Grandpa.

Little Critter wandered around the store. Should he spend his quarters on candy? Or a kite? Or a yo-yo? "Look at those marbles!" said Little Critter.

Little Critter felt the smooth, shiny marbles. The sign said 25 cents each. Little Critter asked Grandpa, "How many cents are in a quarter?"

"Twenty-five, Little Critter," said Grandpa. "You can buy one marble with each quarter."

"I can buy four marbles!" exclaimed Little Critter. He chose a speckled blue marble, a clear marble, an orange-and-green marble, and a bright red marble.

"That will be one dollar," said the store clerk.

"But I only have four quarters!" said Little Critter.

"That's just right," said Grandpa. "Four quarters is the same as one dollar!"

Name ______________________________

Thinking Skills

Directions: Answer the questions about the story.

1. What is the main idea of the story?

____

____

____

2. What things did Little Critter think about buying?

____

____

3. Describe the marbles that Little Critter bought.

____

____

____

____

4. How much did the marbles cost?

____

____

5. What would you have bought at the general store? Why?

____

____

____

Reading Skills

Directions: Write two sentences that describe the picture below.

1. ______________________________

____

2. ______________________________

____

Directions: Circle the word that best completes each sentence about the story. Then, write each word in the blank.

1. Grandma gave Little Critter four ____________.

   quarts queens quarters

2. Little Critter felt the smooth, shiny ____________.

   kites marbles candles

3. Grandma told Little Critter to buy a ____________.

   treat trick trap

A Gift for Grandma and Grandpa

Read to find out what Little Critter gives Grandma and Grandpa.

Little Critter was sitting on the floor playing with his new marbles. Grandpa was taking a nap on the couch. Grandma was sewing.

"Does anyone want to play checkers?" asked Little Critter.

Grandpa snored. Grandma said, "Maybe later."

Little Critter wandered upstairs. *Soon Mom and Dad and Little Sister will come get me. I will miss Grandma and Grandpa, but I will be glad to be home,* Little Critter thought.

Little Critter made a card for Grandma and Grandpa.

Dear Grandma and Grandpa,

I have had fun at the farm. I love the animals. The country fair was fun, too. I liked fishing with you, Grandpa, and baking pies with you, Grandma. I will miss you when I go home, but we can write letters. I am giving you a present, too.

Love,

Little Critter

Later, Little Critter gave his grandparents the card. "Thank you, Little Critter," said Grandma.

"We're going to miss you around here, Little Critter," said Grandpa.

"Close your eyes and put out your hand," said Little Critter.

Little Critter placed a red marble in Grandpa's hand and a speckled blue marble in Grandma's hand.

"Thank you, Little Critter! These pretty marbles are a treasure," said Grandma. "We'll keep them right here in the kitchen window."

Name ______________________________

Thinking Skills

Directions: Answer the questions about the story.

1. What is the main idea of the story?

____

____

____

____

2. What was Grandpa doing?

____

____

3. What was Grandma doing?

____

4. What was Little Critter thinking as he wandered upstairs?

____

____

____

5. What did Little Critter make for Grandma and Grandpa? Why?

____

____

____

____

Reading Skills

Directions: Write two sentences that describe the picture below.

1. ______________________________

____

2. ______________________________

____

Directions: Write a word from the story that rhymes with each word below.

1. measure ____________
2. hard ____________
3. door ____________
4. skies ____________
5. kiss ____________
6. sand ____________
7. making ____________

Pancake Breakfast

Read about what Little Critter wants for breakfast.

Little Critter was outside with Grandpa feeding the animals when Grandma called, "Breakfast is ready!"

Grandma put a tall stack of pancakes in front of Grandpa. She poured coffee for Grandpa and orange juice for Little Critter.

"I'm not that hungry, Grandma," said Little Critter.

"Not hungry?" asked Grandma. "I thought you'd like a special breakfast on your last day here."

"I'll just have some coffee like Grandpa," said Little Critter.

"I didn't know you drank coffee, Little Critter," said Grandma.

"Oh, yes, I like coffee," said Little Critter.

Grandma poured a little coffee into a mug for Little Critter. He took a small sip. Then he spit the bitter coffee out of his mouth into a napkin.

"I guess I don't like this kind," said Little Critter.

"I have something you will like better," said Grandma.

Grandma poured some pancake batter onto the hot griddle. Little Critter watched her flip some funny-shaped pancakes. Soon she gave him two pancakes, one shaped like a letter "L," and the other like a "C."

"'L' is for *Little,*" said Grandma, "and 'C' is for *Critter*. Especially for you."

Little Critter smiled as he put butter and maple syrup on his letters. "Thanks, Grandma. This is a special breakfast."

Name ______________________________

Thinking Skills

Directions: Answer the questions about the story.

1. What was Little Critter doing before breakfast?

____

____

2. What did Grandma give Grandpa and Little Critter to drink?

____

____

____

3. Why do you think that Little Critter wasn't very hungry?

____

____

4. What did Grandma make especially for Little Critter?

____

____

____

____

5. How do you know that Little Critter liked his pancakes?

____

____

Reading Skills

Directions: Write two sentences that describe the picture below.

1. _______________________________

____

2. _______________________________

____

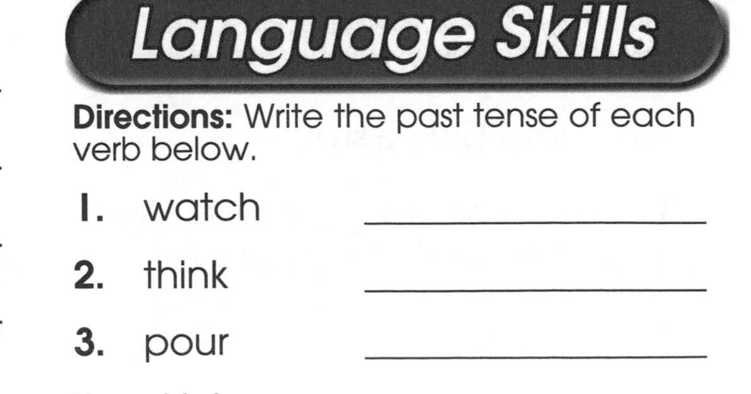

Language Skills

Directions: Write the past tense of each verb below.

1. watch ____________
2. think ____________
3. pour ____________
4. drink ____________
5. give ____________

Little Sister Wants to Have Fun

Find out how Little Critter helps Little Sister have some fun.

When his family arrived, Little Critter told everyone about his visit. "I fed the pigs and the sheep. I rode a horse, and I helped bake a blackberry pie. I went to the general store and the country fair. I ate too much blueberry pie at the fair and got a tummy ache. I know how to take care of goats and how to milk a cow."

"I'm glad you had a good time, Little Critter," said Mrs. Critter.

"I even beat Grandpa at checkers," said Little Critter.

"No fair!" said Little Sister. "You get to do everything just because you're bigger." She folded her arms and frowned.

"Do you want to go see the pond?" Little Critter asked his sister.

"No," said Little Sister.

"Do you want to go look for the turtle that I found?" he asked.

"No," she said.

Little Critter had another idea. "Want to play checkers?"

"Okay," said Little Sister.

Little Critter and Little Sister set up Grandpa's checkerboard. Little Sister said, "These checkers look like cookies!"

"Grandpa made them," said Little Critter.

Little Sister won three games in a row. "This is fun!" she said. "I guess you're a pretty good big brother."

Name ____________________

Thinking Skills

Directions: Answer the questions about the story.

1. List three things that Little Critter told his family about his visit.

____

____

____

2. Why was Little Sister upset? How do you know?

____

____

____

____

3. Why did Little Sister like the checkers game?

____

____

____

4. Why did Little Sister say that Little Critter was a good big brother?

____

____

____

Reading Skills

Directions: Write two sentences that describe the picture below.

1. ____________________

____

2. ____________________

____

Language Skills

Directions: Write an adjective to describe each noun below.

1. __________ Little Sister
2. __________ turtle
3. __________ pond
4. __________ brother

Saying Good-bye to the Farm

Read to find out why Little Critter won't be sad.

It was time for the Critter family to head home. Little Critter walked around the farmyard to say good-bye to all the animals. Little Sister followed him.

They went to the sheep pen first. "Good-bye, sheep!" said Little Critter. "Good-bye, sheep!" said Little Sister.

Then they went to the barn. "Good-bye, Old Kicker and Buttercup," said Little Critter. "Good-bye, Old Kicker and Buttercup," said Little Sister.

"Next time, it will be your turn to visit the farm, Little Sister," said Little Critter.

"I can't wait until next time!" she said.

Little Critter hugged Grandma and Grandpa good-bye. He remembered his good manners. "Thank you for everything, Grandma and Grandpa," said Little Critter.

"Don't look so sad, Little Critter," said Grandpa.

Mrs. Critter said, "I think I can cheer you up, Little Critter. What if Grandma and Grandpa come visit us in a couple of weeks?"

"That would be great! But, what about all the animals?" asked Little Critter.

"We have some kind friends who will feed our animals while we visit you," said Grandma.

"That's good," said Little Critter, "because I don't think we can fit all those animals in our house!"

Name ____________________

Thinking Skills

Directions: Answer the questions about the story.

1. What is the main idea of the story?

____

____

____

2. Who will visit the farm next time?

____

____

3. Why was Little Critter sad?

____

____

____

4. How did Little Critter remember his good manners?

____

____

____

Reading Skills

Directions: Write each group of words in **ABC** order.

1. then ____________________
   they ____________________
   thank ____________________
   those ____________________
   think ____________________

2. sheep ____________________
   said ____________________
   she ____________________
   so ____________________
   sad ____________________

3. head ____________________
   home ____________________
   him ____________________
   hugged ____________________
   his ____________________

Language Skills

Directions: Write a contraction from the story that stands for each pair of words below.

1. do not ____________________
2. can not ____________________
3. that is ____________________

Glad to Be Home

Read to see what Little Critter thinks when he wakes up at home.

When Little Critter got home, he went right to his room. He was glad to see his own bed. He was glad to see his football helmet, his skateboard, and his Super Critter costume. He put his two new marbles on the table next to his bed. They would remind him of the farm until he could visit again.

Mom and Dad came in. "Good night, Little Critter," said Mom. She gave him a hug.

"We're glad you are home," said his dad. "We missed you."

"I missed you, too," said Little Critter, as he climbed into his bed and turned out the light. His room at home was not too dark. It was just right. He dreamed about green and yellow cornfields and chasing furry little lambs. He dreamed about blackberry pie and letter-shaped pancakes.

The next morning when Little Critter woke up, he thought, *Oh, no! There are chores to do! I have to feed the animals! I'm late!* He looked around. He saw that he was home in his own room. He smiled and said, "I can sleep in today!" Little Critter pulled the blankets around him and went back to sleep.

Name ______________________________

Thinking Skills

Directions: Answer the questions about the story.

1. What did Little Critter do when he got home from the farm?

____

2. What did Little Critter dream about?

____

____

____

3. How did Little Critter feel about being in his own room?

____

____

Reading Skills

Directions: Number the sentences **1**, **2**, **3**, and **4** to show what happened first, second, third, and last in the story.

_____ Little Critter said he could sleep in.

_____ Little Critter dreamed about the farm.

_____ Little Critter went right to his room.

_____ Dad said that they all missed Little Critter.

Directions: Write four sentences. Use one word from below in each sentence.

animals	dreamed
costume	remind

1. ______________________________

____

2. ______________________________

____

3. ______________________________

____

4. ______________________________

____

Answer Key

Name ______

Thinking Skills

Directions: Circle the word that best completes each sentence about the story. Then, write the word in the blank.

1. Mom was holding a shovel.
   (shovel) shoe
2. Little Critter and his mom went out to the yard.
   (yard) yarn
3. Little Critter thinks Blue is smart.
   small (smart)

Reading Skills

Directions: Write a sentence that describes the picture on this page.

Sentences will vary

Language Skills

Directions: Write a pronoun that could replace the underlined word or words.

1. Little Critter wants to train his dog. He
2. Mom said the garden was a mess. She
3. Put the shovel away. it

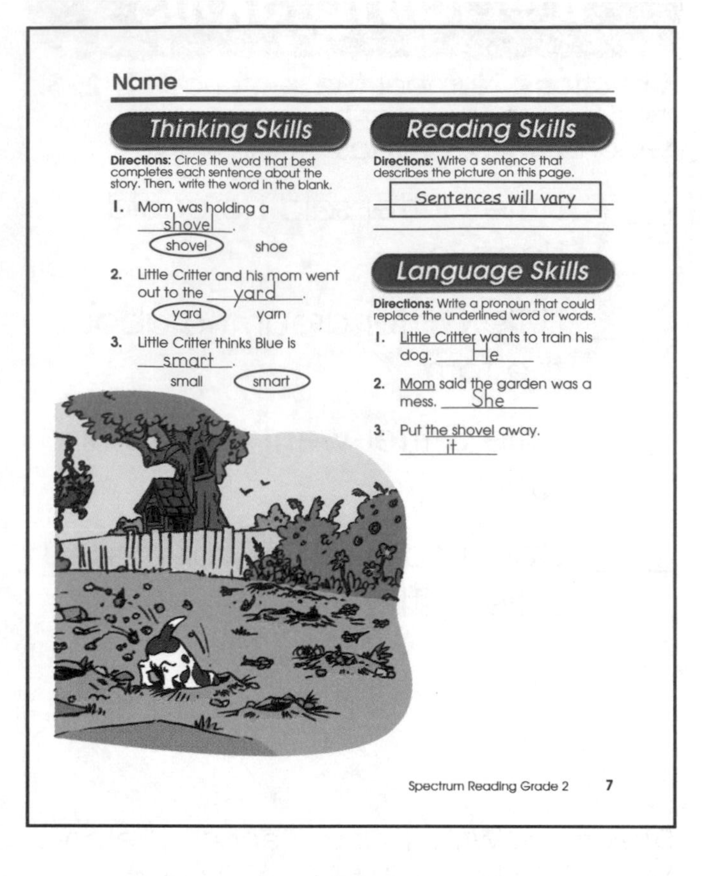

Name ______

Thinking Skills

Directions: Circle the word that best completes each sentence about the story. Then, write the word in the blank.

1. Little Critter and Little Sister helped Mom.
   talked (helped) barked
2. They planted new flowers.
   trees water (flowers)
3. Blue got everyone wet.
   muddy happy (wet)
4. Little Critter hugged his dog.
   kissed (hugged) petted

Reading Skills

Directions: Write a sentence that tells about Blue.

Sentences will vary

Directions: Write a word from the story that rhymes with each word below.

1. book shook
2. hug dug
3. walk talk

Name ______

Thinking Skills

Directions: Answer the questions about the story.

1. Why was the gate open?
   Little Critter went to get the mail.
2. Tell one thing that Blue did after he ran through the gate.
   Blue jumped over a fence.
3. Why was Mrs. Crabtree frowning?
   She was frowning because Little Critter ran into her.

Reading Skills

Directions: Number the sentences **1**, **2**, and **3** to show what happened first, next, and last in the story.

2 Blue ran through the open gate.

3 Little Critter chased Blue.

1 Little Critter looked at the mail.

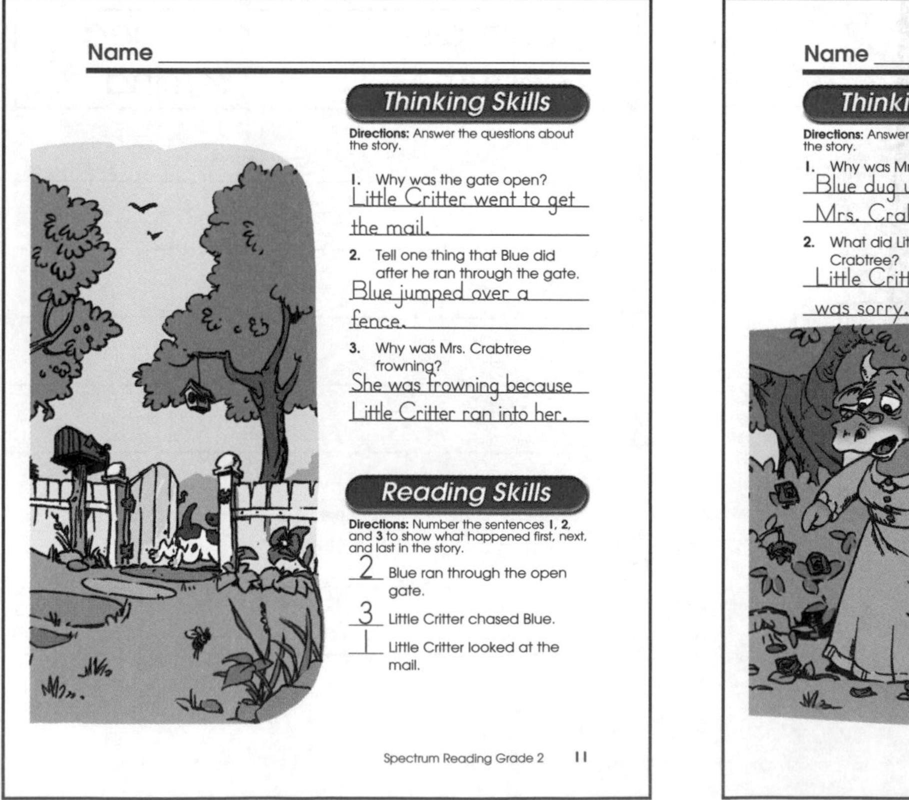

Name ______

Thinking Skills

Directions: Answer the questions about the story.

1. Why was Mrs. Crabtree angry?
   Blue dug up Mrs. Crabtree's roses.
2. What did Little Critter tell Mrs. Crabtree?
   Little Critter said he was sorry.

Reading Skills

Directions: Write the words from the story in **ABC** order.

1. bank bank
2. yard red
3. red yard

Language Skills

Directions: Circle each **action word** below.

dog (walk) money (dig) (say)

Answer Key

Name

Thinking Skills

Directions: Answer the questions about the story.

1. What is the main idea of the story?
   Little Critter's friends gave their money to help pay for the roses.
2. How much money did Little Critter have in his piggy bank?
   $2.23
3. What are your ideas to earn the extra money?
   Answers will vary

Reading Skills

Examples:

1.	rest	best	vest
2.	roses	noses	hoses
3.	think	drink	wink
4.	same	game	tame
5.	bill	will	fill
6.	bet	wet	met

Spectrum Reading Grade 2 15

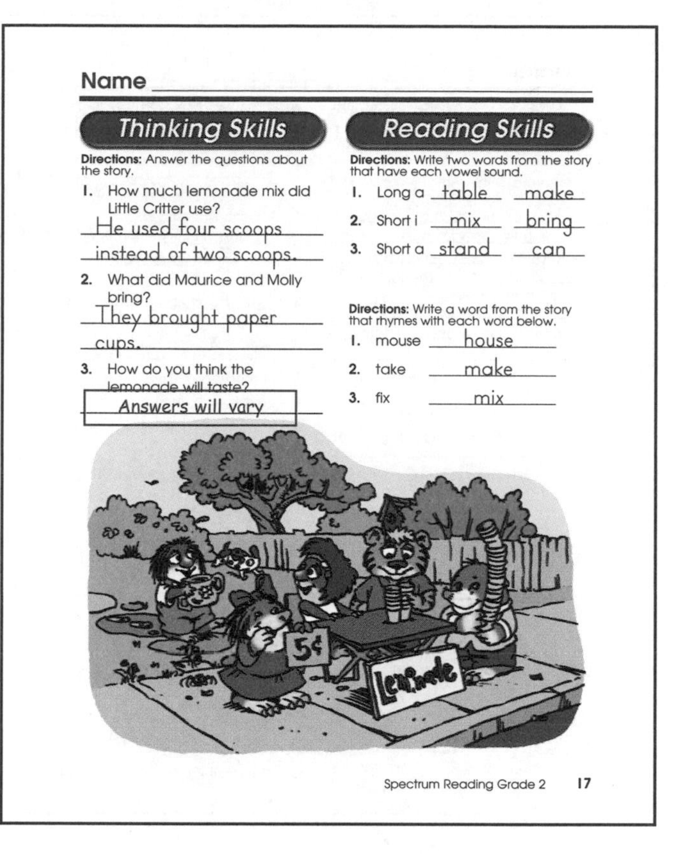

Name

Thinking Skills

Directions: Answer the questions about the story.

1. How much lemonade mix did Little Critter use?
   He used four scoops instead of two scoops.
2. What did Maurice and Molly bring?
   They brought paper cups.
3. How do you think the lemonade will taste?
   Answers will vary

Reading Skills

Directions: Write two words from the story that have each vowel sound.

1. Long a table make
2. Short i mix bring
3. Short a stand can

Directions: Write a word from the story that rhymes with each word below.

1. mouse house
2. take make
3. fix mix

Spectrum Reading Grade 2 17

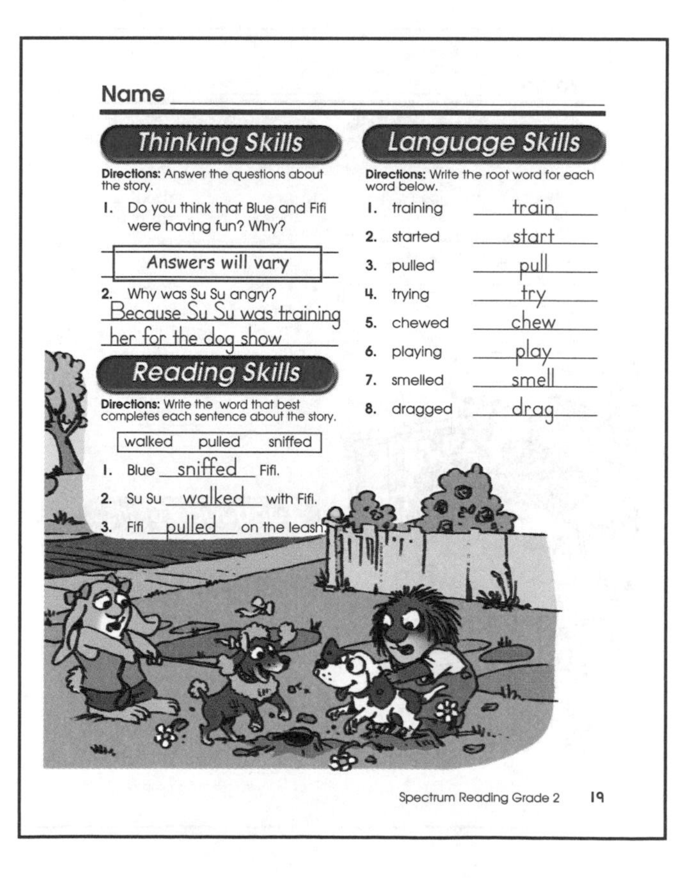

Name

Thinking Skills

Directions: Answer the questions about the story.

1. Do you think that Blue and Fifi were having fun? Why?
   Answers will vary
2. Why was Su Su angry?
   Because Su Su was training her for the dog show

Reading Skills

Directions: Write the word that best completes each sentence about the story.

walked pulled sniffed

1. Blue sniffed Fifi.
2. Su Su walked with Fifi.
3. Fifi pulled on the leash.

Language Skills

Directions: Write the root word for each word below.

1. training train
2. started start
3. pulled pull
4. trying try
5. chewed chew
6. playing play
7. smelled smell
8. dragged drag

Spectrum Reading Grade 2 19

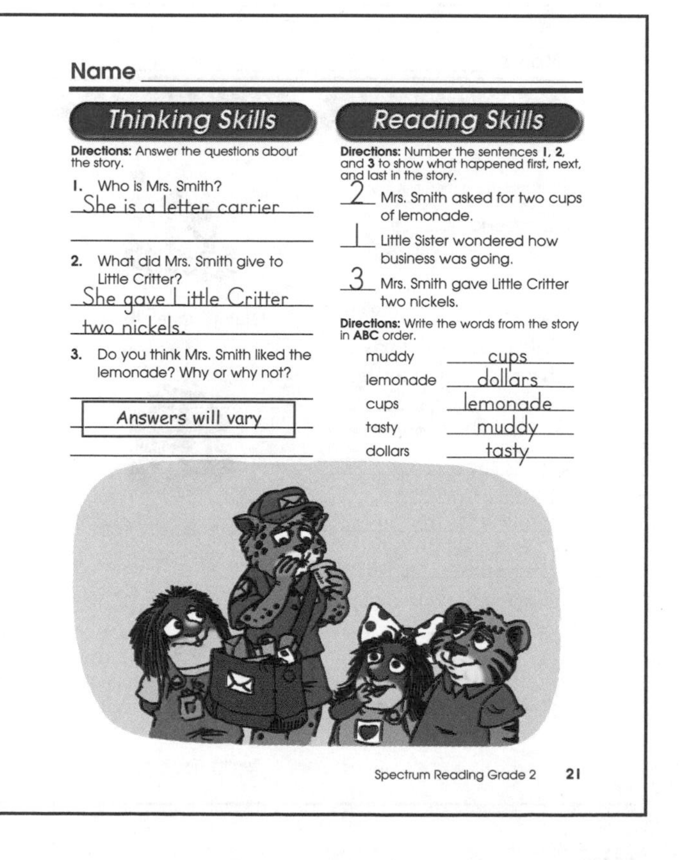

Name

Thinking Skills

Directions: Answer the questions about the story.

1. Who is Mrs. Smith?
   She is a letter carrier
2. What did Mrs. Smith give to Little Critter?
   She gave Little Critter two nickels.
3. Do you think Mrs. Smith liked the lemonade? Why or why not?
   Answers will vary

Reading Skills

Directions: Number the sentences 1, 2, and 3 to show what happened first, next, and last in the story.

2 Mrs. Smith asked for two cups of lemonade.

1 Little Sister wondered how business was going.

3 Mrs. Smith gave Little Critter two nickels.

Directions: Write the words from the story in ABC order.

muddy	cups
lemonade	dollars
cups	lemonade
tasty	muddy
dollars	tasty

Spectrum Reading Grade 2 21

Answer Key

Name

Thinking Skills

Directions: Answer the questions about the story.

1. What is the main idea of the story?
   They don't make much money selling lemonade so they decide to go into town tomorrow.
2. What did Mr. Critter say about the lemonade?
   Mr. Critter said the lemonade was very tangy.
3. What did Tiger think they should do?
   Tiger thought they should go into town.

Reading Skills

Directions: Write the word that best completes each sentence about the story.

bought counted thanked

1. Mr. and Mrs. Critter bought some lemonade.
2. Little Critter thanked his friends.
3. They counted the coins in the cup.

Directions: Write a word from the story that means the **opposite** of each word below.

1. none all
2. cold hot
3. short long

Spectrum Reading Grade 2 23

Name

Thinking Skills

Directions: Answer the questions about the story.

1. What is the main idea of the story?
   Little Critter decided to enter Blue in a dog show.
2. Why does Gabby want to train Blue for the show?
   She has a book about training dogs and thinks Blue can be trained.
3. Do you think that Gabby can train Blue? Why or why not?
   Answers will vary

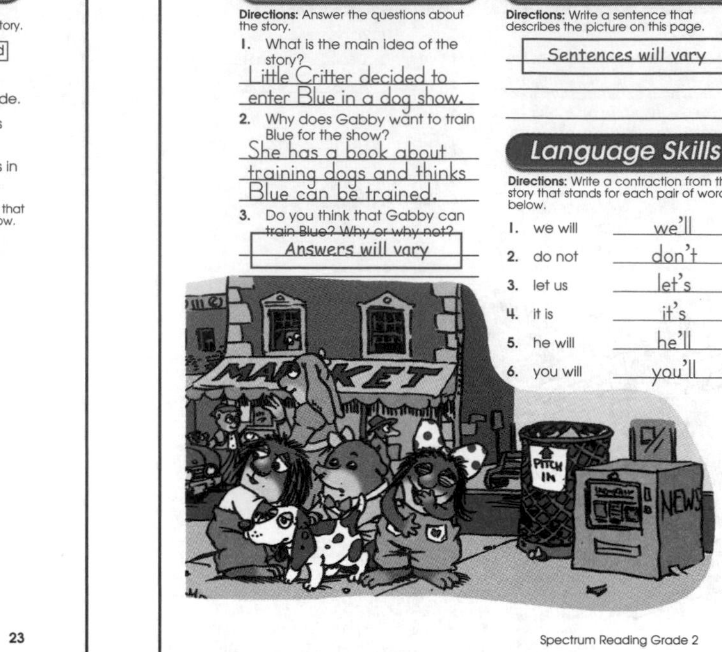

Reading Skills

Directions: Write a sentence that describes the picture on this page.

Sentences will vary

Language Skills

Directions: Write a contraction from the story that stands for each pair of words below.

1. we will we'll
2. do not don't
3. let us let's
4. it is it's
5. he will he'll
6. you will you'll

Spectrum Reading Grade 2 25

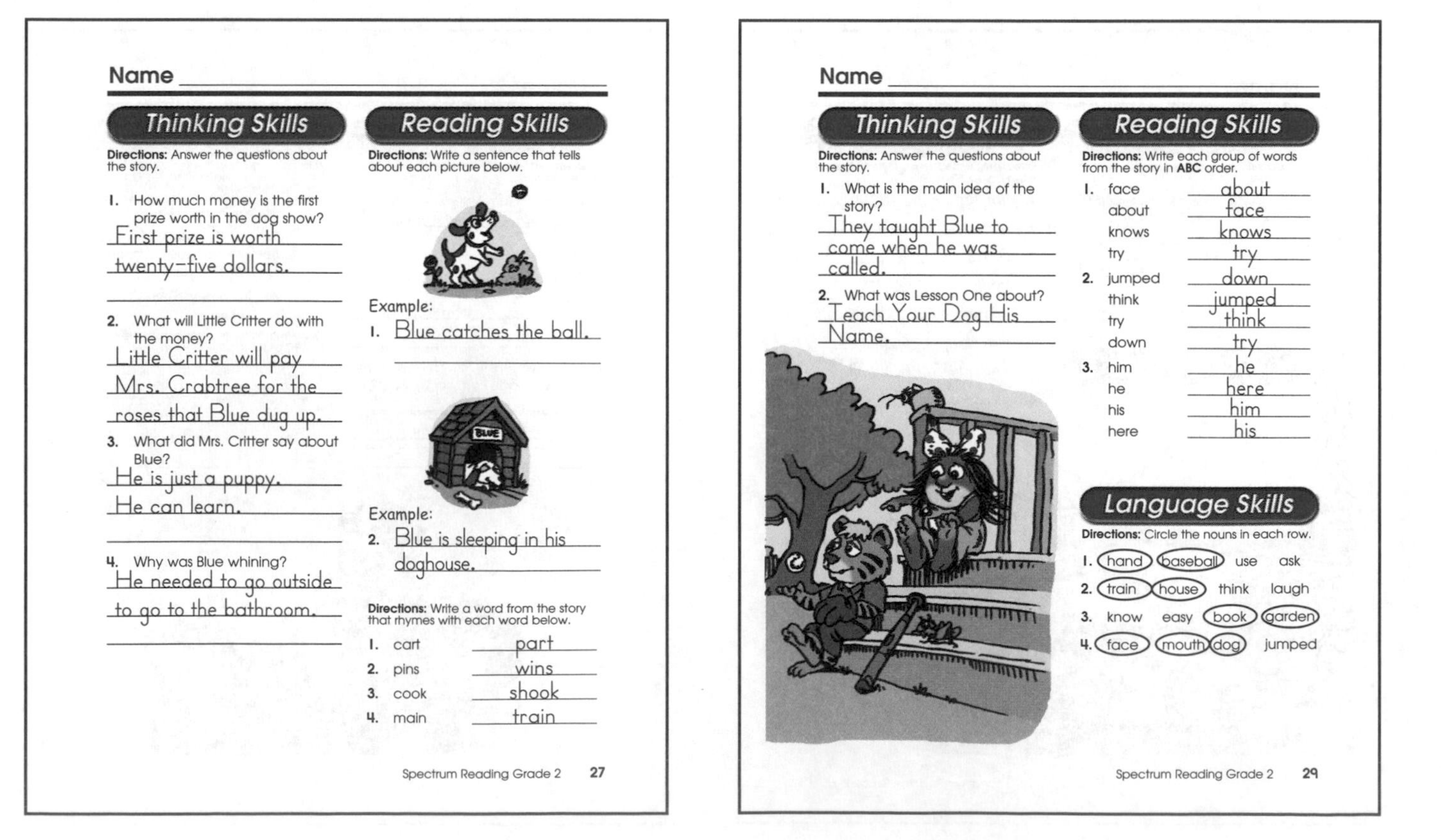

Name

Thinking Skills

Directions: Answer the questions about the story.

1. How much money is the first prize worth in the dog show?
   First prize is worth twenty-five dollars.
2. What will Little Critter do with the money?
   Little Critter will pay Mrs. Crabtree for the roses that Blue dug up.
3. What did Mrs. Critter say about Blue?
   He is just a puppy. He can learn.
4. Why was Blue whining?
   He needed to go outside to go to the bathroom.

Reading Skills

Directions: Write a sentence that tells about each picture below.

Example:
1. Blue catches the ball.

Example:
2. Blue is sleeping in his doghouse.

Directions: Write a word from the story that rhymes with each word below.

1. cart part
2. pins wins
3. cook shook
4. main train

Spectrum Reading Grade 2 27

Name

Thinking Skills

Directions: Answer the questions about the story.

1. What is the main idea of the story?
   They taught Blue to come when he was called.
2. What was Lesson One about?
   Teach Your Dog His Name.

Reading Skills

Directions: Write each group of words from the story in **ABC** order.

1. face — about; about — face; knows — knows; try — try
2. jumped — down; think — jumped; try — think; down — try
3. him — he; he — here; his — him; here — his

Language Skills

Directions: Circle the nouns in each row.

1. (hand) (baseball) use ask
2. (train) (house) think laugh
3. know easy (book) (garden)
4. (face) (mouth) (dog) jumped

Spectrum Reading Grade 2 29

Answer Key

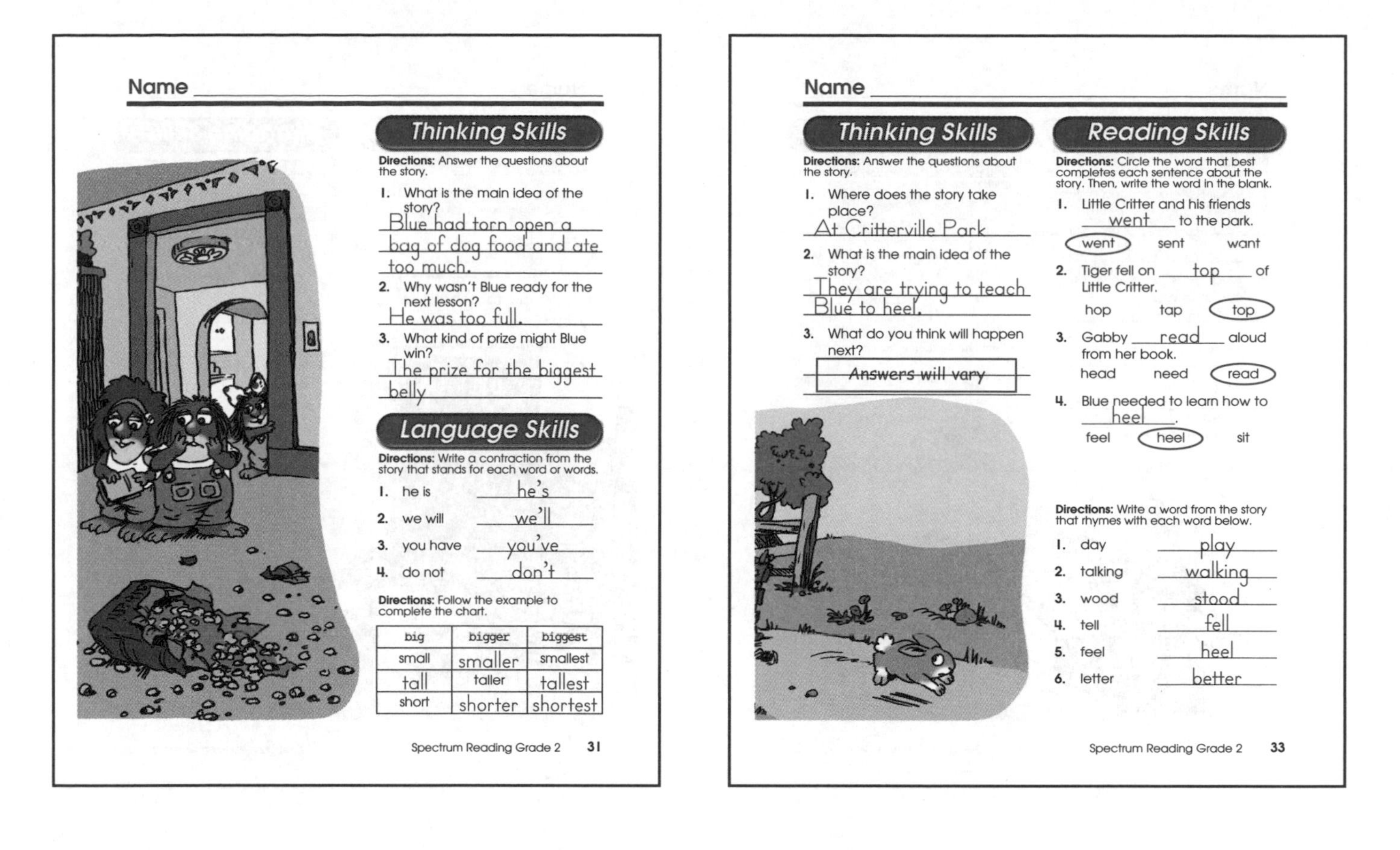

Name

Thinking Skills

Directions: Answer the questions about the story.

1. What is the main idea of the story?
   Blue had torn open a bag of dog food and ate too much.
2. Why wasn't Blue ready for the next lesson?
   He was too full.
3. What kind of prize might Blue win?
   The prize for the biggest belly

Language Skills

Directions: Write a contraction from the story that stands for each word or words.

1. he is he's
2. we will we'll
3. you have you've
4. do not don't

Directions: Follow the example to complete the chart.

big	bigger	biggest
small	smaller	smallest
tall	taller	tallest
short	shorter	shortest

Spectrum Reading Grade 2 31

Name

Thinking Skills

Directions: Answer the questions about the story.

1. Where does the story take place?
   At Critterville Park
2. What is the main idea of the story?
   They are trying to teach Blue to heel.
3. What do you think will happen next?
   Answers will vary

Reading Skills

Directions: Circle the word that best completes each sentence about the story. Then, write the word in the blank.

1. Little Critter and his friends went to the park.
   (went) sent want
2. Tiger fell on top of Little Critter.
   hop tap (top)
3. Gabby read aloud from her book.
   head need (read)
4. Blue needed to learn how to heel.
   feel (heel) sit

Directions: Write a word from the story that rhymes with each word below.

1. day play
2. talking walking
3. wood stood
4. tell fell
5. feel heel
6. letter better

Spectrum Reading Grade 2 33

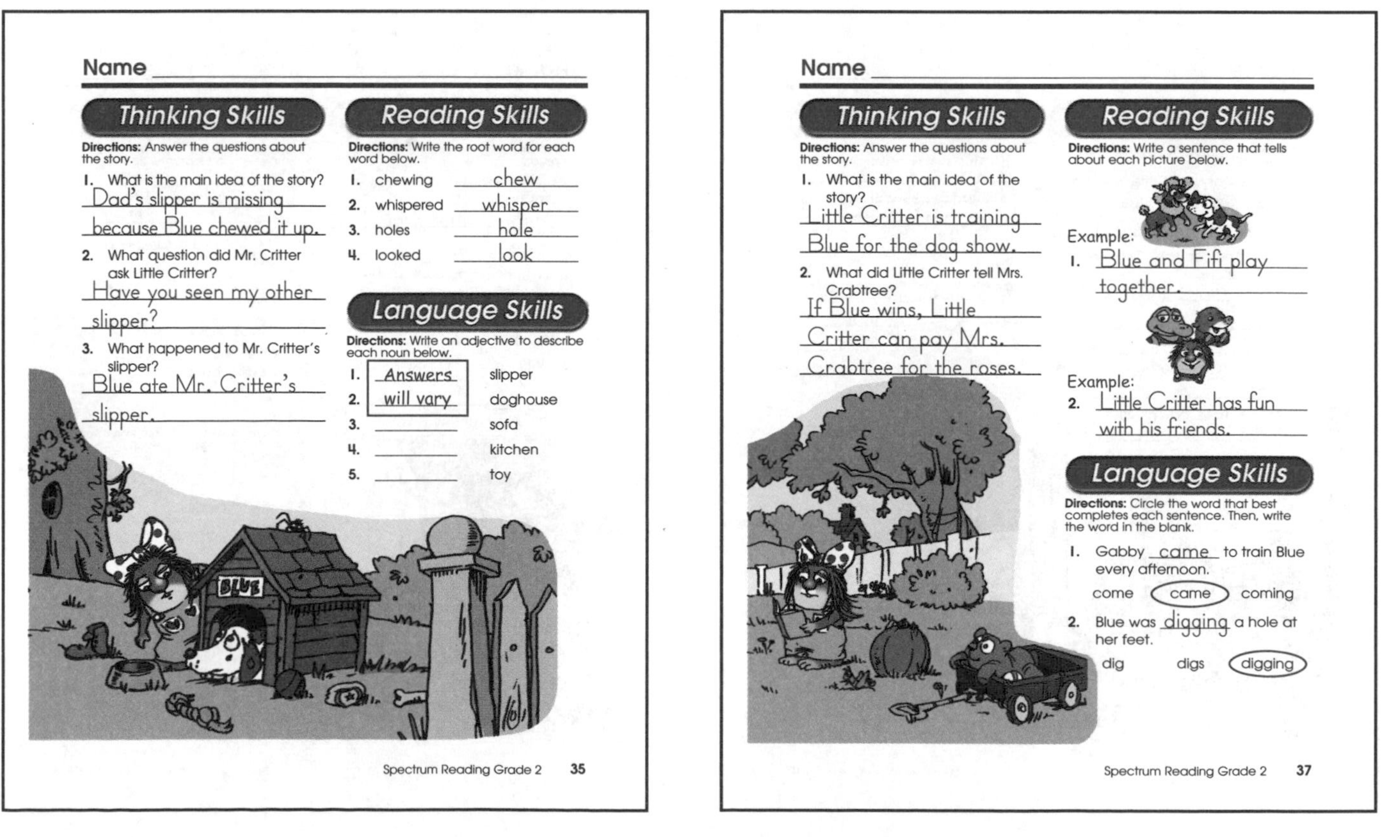

Name

Thinking Skills

Directions: Answer the questions about the story.

1. What is the main idea of the story?
   Dad's slipper is missing because Blue chewed it up.
2. What question did Mr. Critter ask Little Critter?
   Have you seen my other slipper?
3. What happened to Mr. Critter's slipper?
   Blue ate Mr. Critter's slipper.

Reading Skills

Directions: Write the root word for each word below.

1. chewing chew
2. whispered whisper
3. holes hole
4. looked look

Language Skills

Directions: Write an adjective to describe each noun below.

1. Answers slipper
2. will vary doghouse
3. sofa
4. kitchen
5. toy

Spectrum Reading Grade 2 35

Name

Thinking Skills

Directions: Answer the questions about the story.

1. What is the main idea of the story?
   Little Critter is training Blue for the dog show.
2. What did Little Critter tell Mrs. Crabtree?
   If Blue wins, Little Critter can pay Mrs. Crabtree for the roses.

Reading Skills

Directions: Write a sentence that tells about each picture below.

Example:
1. Blue and Fifi play together.

Example:
2. Little Critter has fun with his friends.

Language Skills

Directions: Circle the word that best completes each sentence. Then, write the word in the blank.

1. Gabby came to train Blue every afternoon.
   come (came) coming
2. Blue was digging a hole at her feet.
   dig digs (digging)

Spectrum Reading Grade 2 37

Answer Key

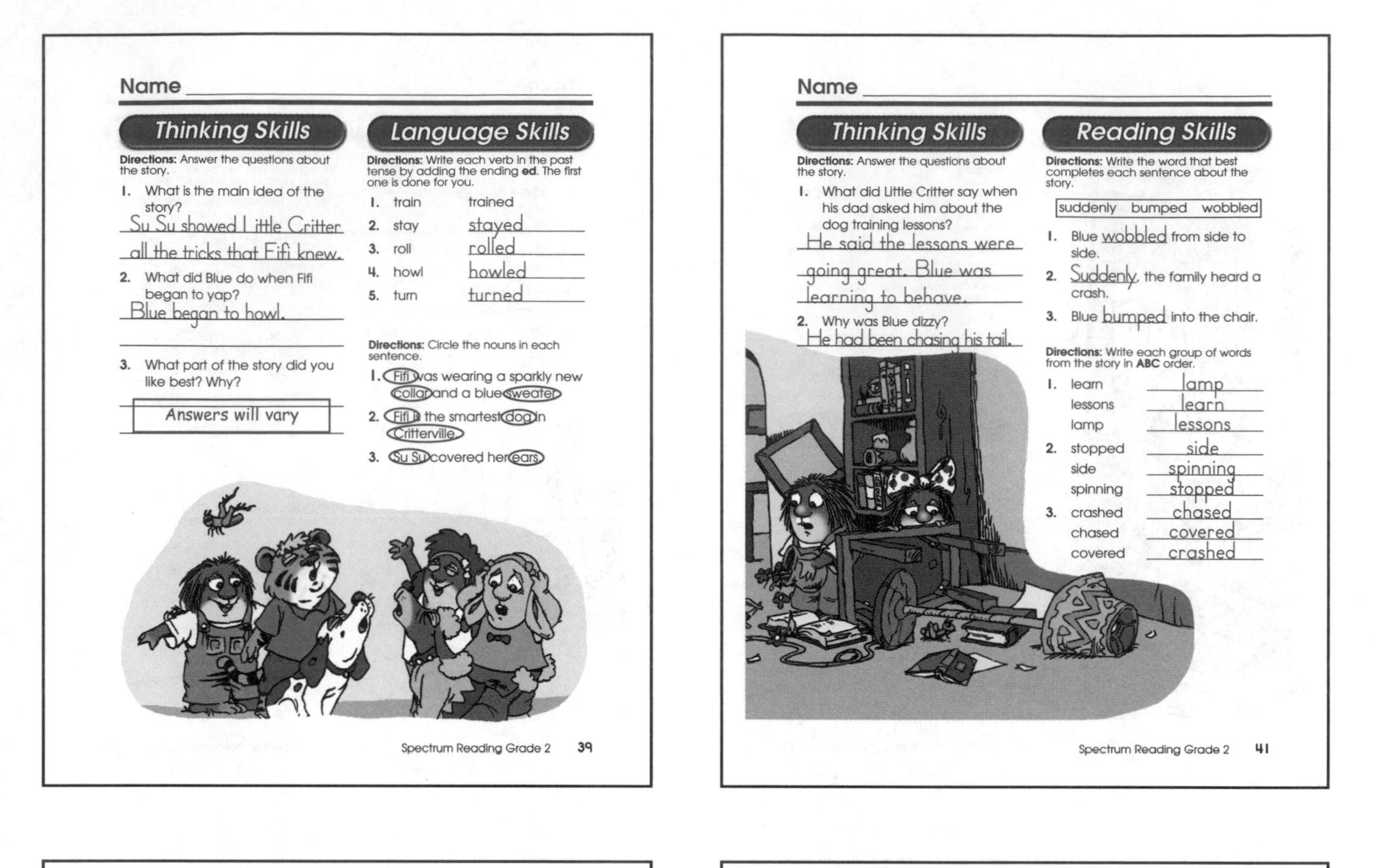

Name

Thinking Skills

Directions: Answer the questions about the story.

1. What is the main idea of the story?
   Su Su showed Little Critter all the tricks that Fifi knew.
2. What did Blue do when Fifi began to yap?
   Blue began to howl.
3. What part of the story did you like best? Why?
   Answers will vary

Language Skills

Directions: Write each verb in the past tense by adding the ending **ed**. The first one is done for you.

1. train trained
2. stay stayed
3. roll rolled
4. howl howled
5. turn turned

Directions: Circle the nouns in each sentence.

1. (Fifi) was wearing a sparkly new (collar) and a blue (sweater).
2. (Fifi) is the smartest (dog) in (Critterville).
3. (Su Su) covered her (ears).

Spectrum Reading Grade 2 39

Name

Thinking Skills

Directions: Answer the questions about the story.

1. What did Little Critter say when his dad asked him about the dog training lessons?
   He said the lessons were going great. Blue was learning to behave.
2. Why was Blue dizzy?
   He had been chasing his tail.

Reading Skills

Directions: Write the word that best completes each sentence about the story.

suddenly bumped wobbled

1. Blue wobbled from side to side.
2. Suddenly, the family heard a crash.
3. Blue bumped into the chair.

Directions: Write each group of words from the story in **ABC** order.

1. learn, lessons, lamp — lamp, learn, lessons
2. stopped, side, spinning — side, spinning, stopped
3. crashed, chased, covered — chased, covered, crashed

Spectrum Reading Grade 2 41

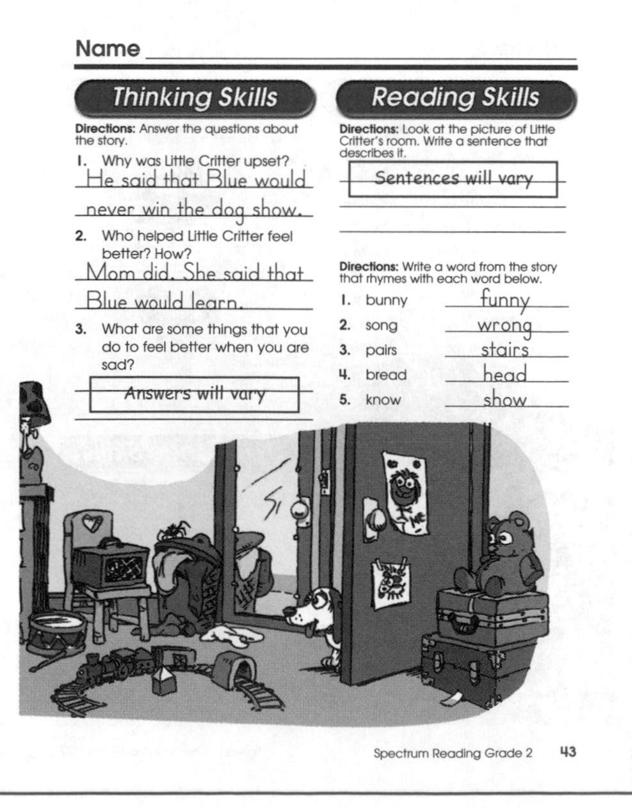

Name

Thinking Skills

Directions: Answer the questions about the story.

1. Why was Little Critter upset?
   He said that Blue would never win the dog show.
2. Who helped Little Critter feel better? How?
   Mom did. She said that Blue would learn.
3. What are some things that you do to feel better when you are sad?
   Answers will vary

Reading Skills

Directions: Look at the picture of Little Critter's room. Write a sentence that describes it.

Sentences will vary

Directions: Write a word from the story that rhymes with each word below.

1. bunny funny
2. song wrong
3. pairs stairs
4. bread head
5. know show

Spectrum Reading Grade 2 43

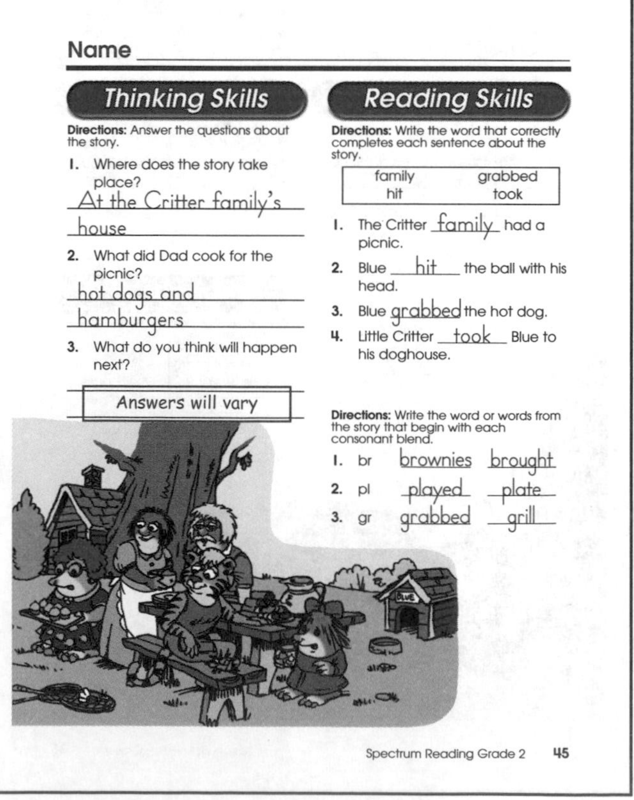

Name

Thinking Skills

Directions: Answer the questions about the story.

1. Where does the story take place?
   At the Critter family's house
2. What did Dad cook for the picnic?
   hot dogs and hamburgers
3. What do you think will happen next?
   Answers will vary

Reading Skills

Directions: Write the word that correctly completes each sentence about the story.

family grabbed hit took

1. The Critter family had a picnic.
2. Blue hit the ball with his head.
3. Blue grabbed the hot dog.
4. Little Critter took Blue to his doghouse.

Directions: Write the word or words from the story that begin with each consonant blend.

1. br brownies brought
2. pl played plate
3. gr grabbed grill

Spectrum Reading Grade 2 45

Answer Key

Name

Thinking Skills

Directions: Answer the questions about the story.

1. What did Gabby want to teach Blue?
   She wanted to teach Blue how to shake hands.
2. After reading this story, do you think Blue will win the dog show? Why or why not?
   Answers will vary

Reading Skills

Directions: Circle the word that best completes each sentence. Then, write the word in the blank.

1. We're going to teach Blue how to shake hands.
   take (teach) tear
2. Blue wagged his tail and barked.
   train take (tail)
3. Little Critter quickly gave Blue a piece of hot dog.
   game (gave) gate

Language Skills

Directions: Write a pronoun from below to replace the underlined words.

He They She

1. Maurice and Molly are friends with Little Critter. They
2. Blue is learning new tricks. He
3. Gabby brings her dog training book each day. She

Spectrum Reading Grade 2 47

Name

Thinking Skills

Directions: Answer the questions about the story.

1. What does Mrs. Critter want to make for lunch?
   She wants to make tuna fish sandwiches.
2. What does Little Sister want to make for lunch?
   She wants to make jelly and potato chip sandwiches.

Reading Skills

Directions: Number the sentences 1, 2, and 3 to show what happened first, next, and last in the story.

2 Little Critter doesn't think Mrs. Crabtree will be his friend.
3 Mrs. Critter wanted to make tuna fish sandwiches.
1 Mrs. Critter had an idea.

Directions: Write the word that best completes each sentence about the story.

idea sandwiches friend everyone

1. We will have sandwiches for lunch.
2. Mrs. Critter told them her idea.
3. Everyone likes tuna fish.
4. She won't be my friend.

Spectrum Reading Grade 2 49

Name

Thinking Skills

Directions: Answer the questions about the story.

1. What did Blue bring to Mrs. Crabtree?
   Little Sister's doll, Little Critter's pajamas, other toys, and a towel
2. How do you think Mrs. Crabtree feels about Blue now?
   Answers will vary

Reading Skills

Examples:

1. lunch bunch crunch
2. came tame fame
3. roses noses hoses
4. how now cow
5. back jack tack
6. keep sweep peep

Directions: Write a sentence that describes the picture on this page.

Sentences will vary

Spectrum Reading Grade 2 51

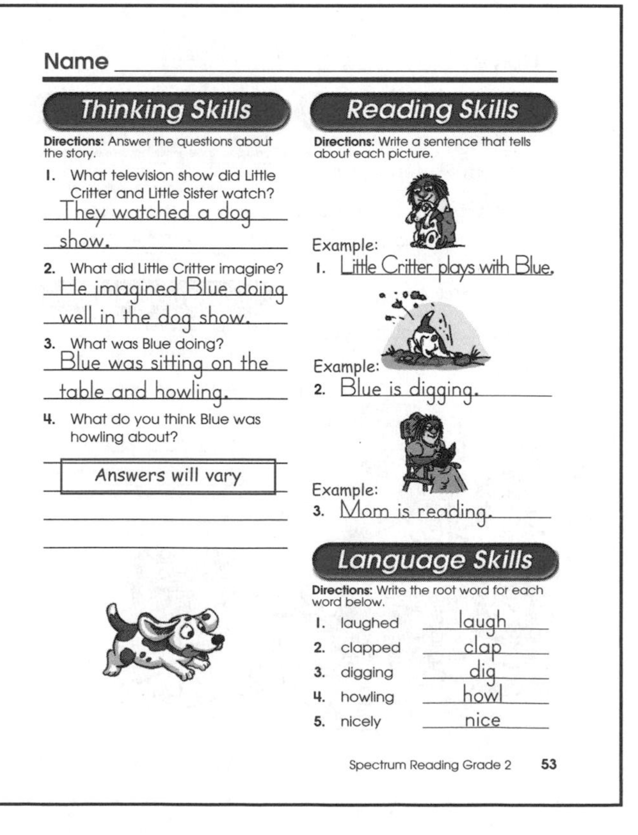

Name

Thinking Skills

Directions: Answer the questions about the story.

1. What television show did Little Critter and Little Sister watch?
   They watched a dog show.
2. What did Little Critter imagine?
   He imagined Blue doing well in the dog show.
3. What was Blue doing?
   Blue was sitting on the table and howling.
4. What do you think Blue was howling about?
   Answers will vary

Reading Skills

Directions: Write a sentence that tells about each picture.

Example:
1. Little Critter plays with Blue.

Example:
2. Blue is digging.

Example:
3. Mom is reading.

Language Skills

Directions: Write the root word for each word below.

1. laughed laugh
2. clapped clap
3. digging dig
4. howling howl
5. nicely nice

Spectrum Reading Grade 2 53

Answer Key

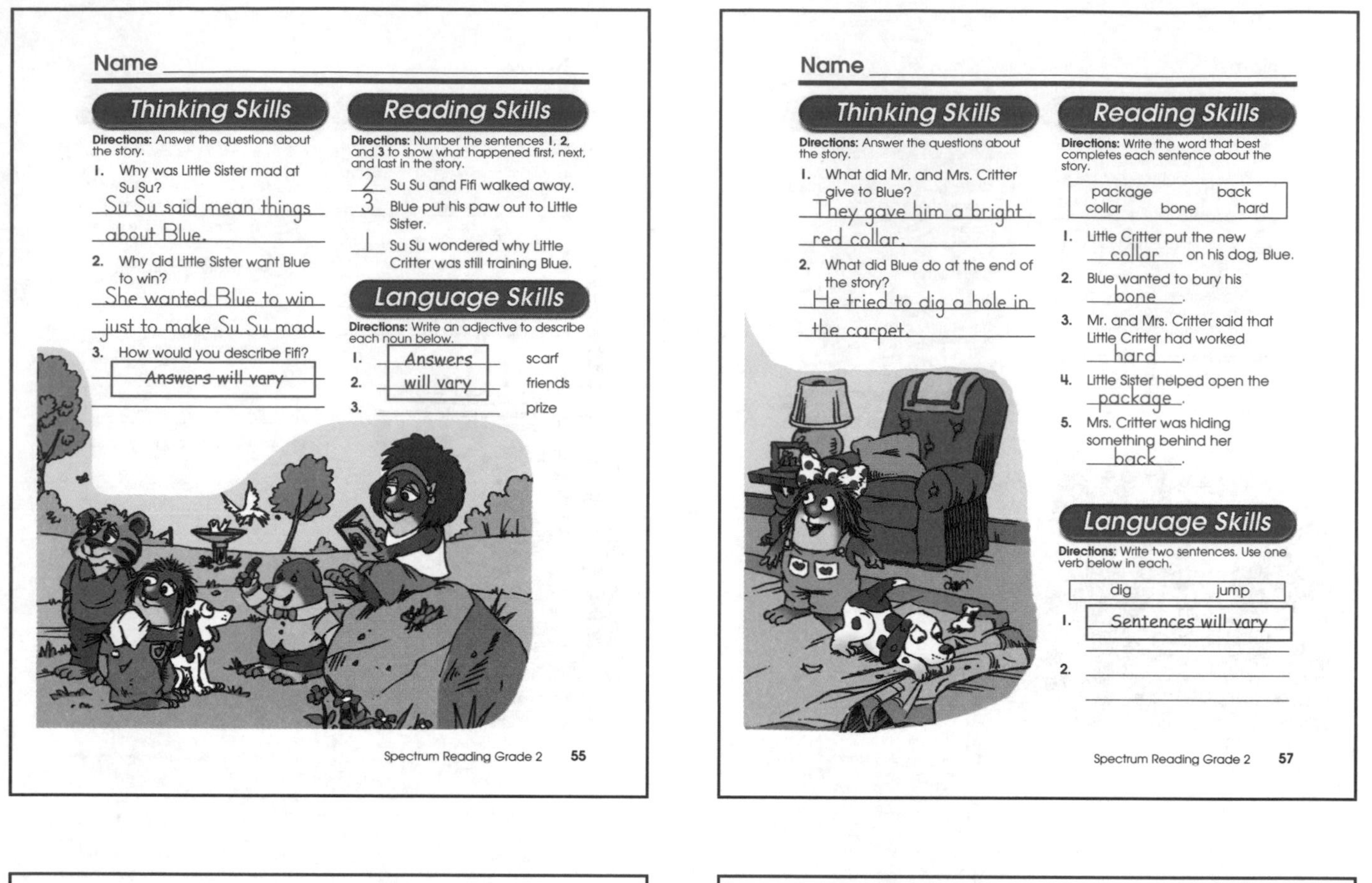

Name

Thinking Skills

Directions: Answer the questions about the story.

1. Why was Little Sister mad at Su Su?
   Su Su said mean things about Blue.
2. Why did Little Sister want Blue to win?
   She wanted Blue to win just to make Su Su mad.
3. How would you describe Fifi?
   Answers will vary

Reading Skills

Directions: Number the sentences **1**, **2**, and **3** to show what happened first, next, and last in the story.

2 Su Su and Fifi walked away.
3 Blue put his paw out to Little Sister.
1 Su Su wondered why Little Critter was still training Blue.

Language Skills

Directions: Write an adjective to describe each noun below.

1. Answers scarf
2. will vary friends
3. prize

Spectrum Reading Grade 2 55

Name

Thinking Skills

Directions: Answer the questions about the story.

1. What did Mr. and Mrs. Critter give to Blue?
   They gave him a bright red collar.
2. What did Blue do at the end of the story?
   He tried to dig a hole in the carpet.

Reading Skills

Directions: Write the word that best completes each sentence about the story.

package back collar bone hard

1. Little Critter put the new collar on his dog, Blue.
2. Blue wanted to bury his bone.
3. Mr. and Mrs. Critter said that Little Critter had worked hard.
4. Little Sister helped open the package.
5. Mrs. Critter was hiding something behind her back.

Language Skills

Directions: Write two sentences. Use one verb below in each.

dig jump

1. Sentences will vary
2.

Spectrum Reading Grade 2 57

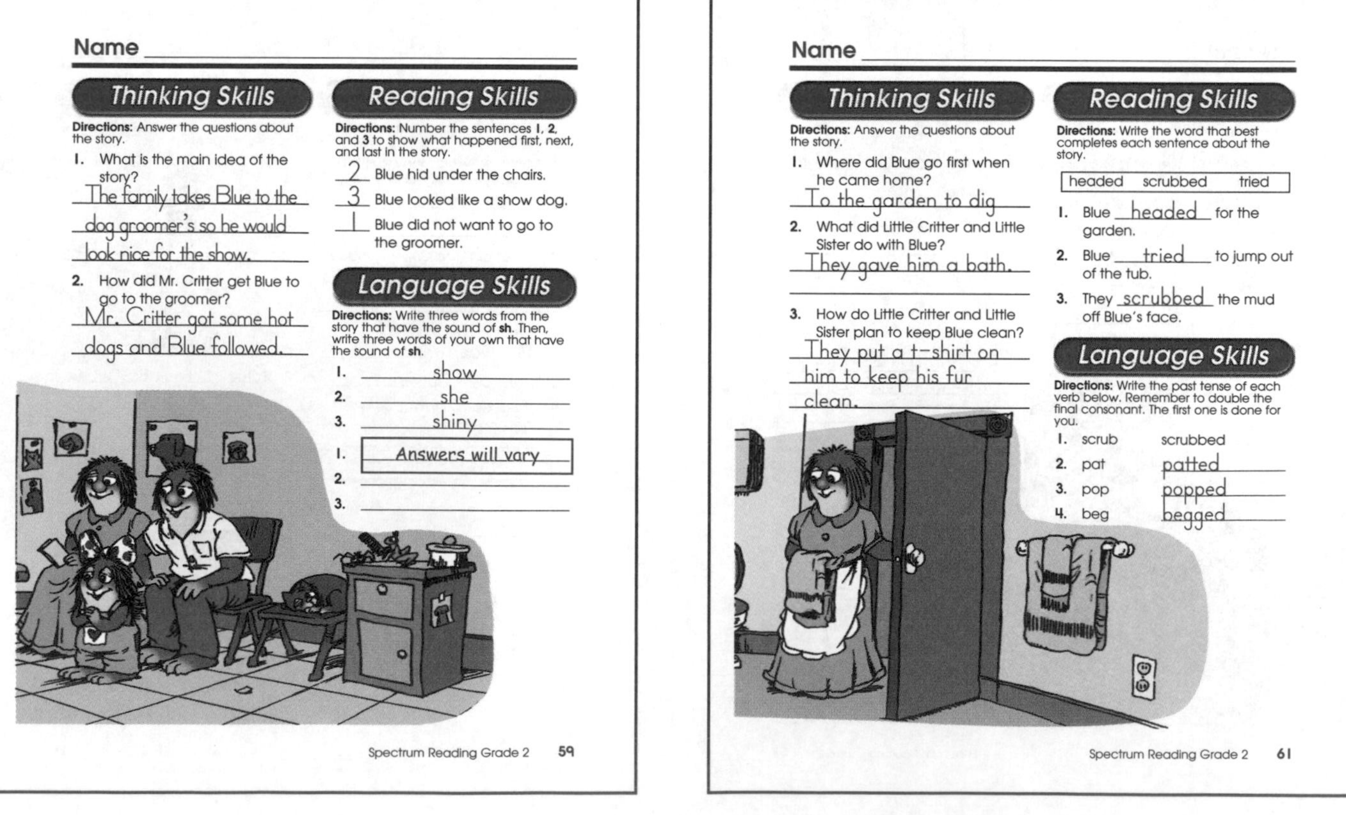

Name

Thinking Skills

Directions: Answer the questions about the story.

1. What is the main idea of the story?
   The family takes Blue to the dog groomer's so he would look nice for the show.
2. How did Mr. Critter get Blue to go to the groomer?
   Mr. Critter got some hot dogs and Blue followed.

Reading Skills

Directions: Number the sentences **1**, **2**, and **3** to show what happened first, next, and last in the story.

2 Blue hid under the chairs.
3 Blue looked like a show dog.
1 Blue did not want to go to the groomer.

Language Skills

Directions: Write three words from the story that have the sound of **sh**. Then, write three words of your own that have the sound of **sh**.

1. show
2. she
3. shiny

1. Answers will vary
2.
3.

Spectrum Reading Grade 2 59

Name

Thinking Skills

Directions: Answer the questions about the story.

1. Where did Blue go first when he came home?
   To the garden to dig
2. What did Little Critter and Little Sister do with Blue?
   They gave him a bath.
3. How do Little Critter and Little Sister plan to keep Blue clean?
   They put a t-shirt on him to keep his fur clean.

Reading Skills

Directions: Write the word that best completes each sentence about the story.

headed scrubbed tried

1. Blue headed for the garden.
2. Blue tried to jump out of the tub.
3. They scrubbed the mud off Blue's face.

Language Skills

Directions: Write the past tense of each verb below. Remember to double the final consonant. The first one is done for you.

1. scrub scrubbed
2. pat patted
3. pop popped
4. beg begged

Spectrum Reading Grade 2 61

Answer Key

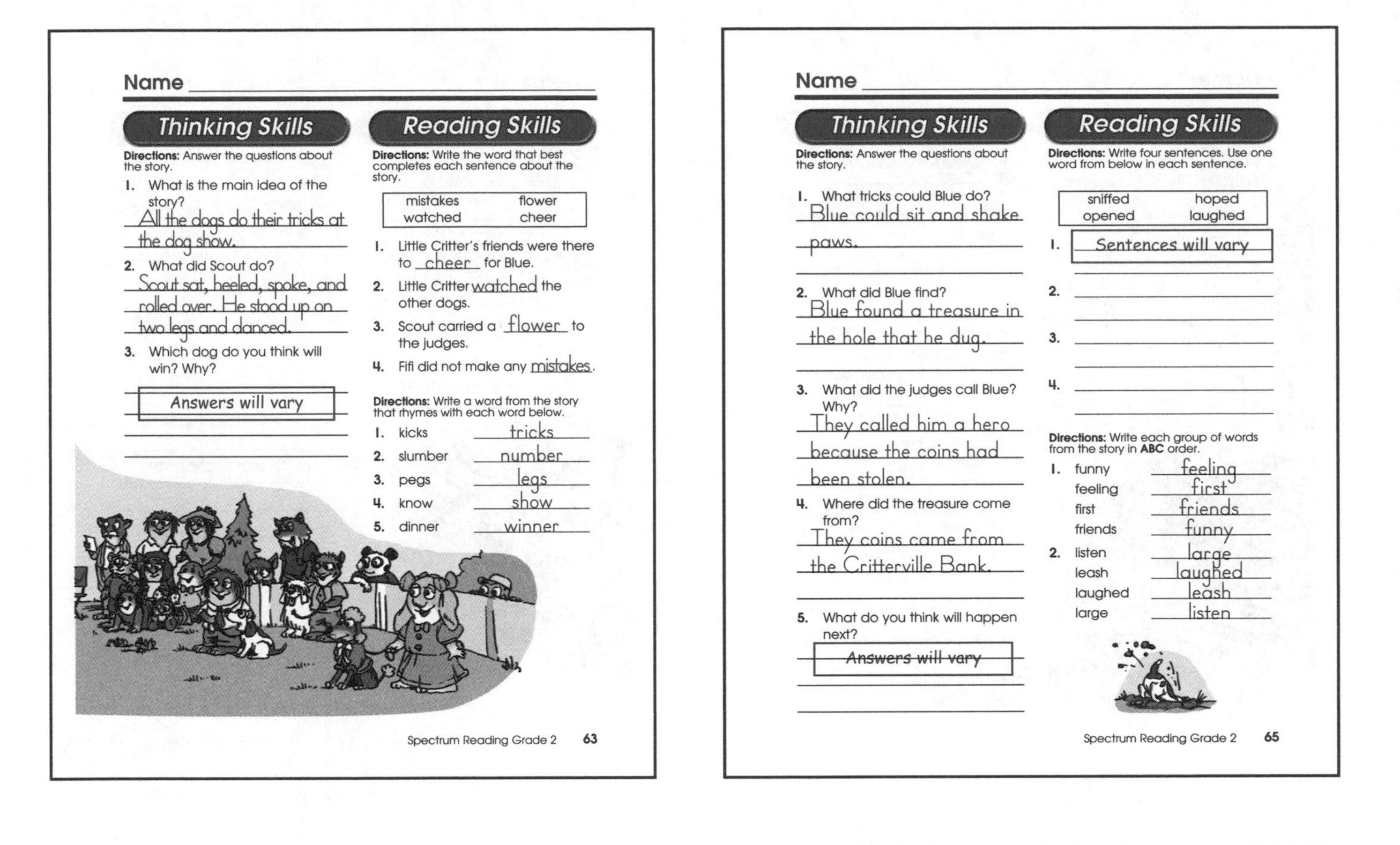

Name

Thinking Skills

Directions: Answer the questions about the story.

1. What is the main idea of the story?
   All the dogs do their tricks at the dog show.
2. What did Scout do?
   Scout sat, heeled, spoke, and rolled over. He stood up on two legs and danced.
3. Which dog do you think will win? Why?
   Answers will vary

Reading Skills

Directions: Write the word that best completes each sentence about the story.

mistakes	flower
watched	cheer

1. Little Critter's friends were there to cheer for Blue.
2. Little Critter watched the other dogs.
3. Scout carried a flower to the judges.
4. Fifi did not make any mistakes.

Directions: Write a word from the story that rhymes with each word below.

1. kicks — tricks
2. slumber — number
3. pegs — legs
4. know — show
5. dinner — winner

Spectrum Reading Grade 2 63

Name

Thinking Skills

Directions: Answer the questions about the story.

1. What tricks could Blue do?
   Blue could sit and shake paws.
2. What did Blue find?
   Blue found a treasure in the hole that he dug.
3. What did the judges call Blue? Why?
   They called him a hero because the coins had been stolen.
4. Where did the treasure come from?
   They coins came from the Critterville Bank.
5. What do you think will happen next?
   Answers will vary

Reading Skills

Directions: Write four sentences. Use one word from below in each sentence.

sniffed	hoped
opened	laughed

1. Sentences will vary
2.
3.
4.

Directions: Write each group of words from the story in **ABC** order.

1. funny, feeling, first, friends — feeling, first, friends, funny
2. listen, leash, laughed, large — large, laughed, leash, listen

Spectrum Reading Grade 2 65

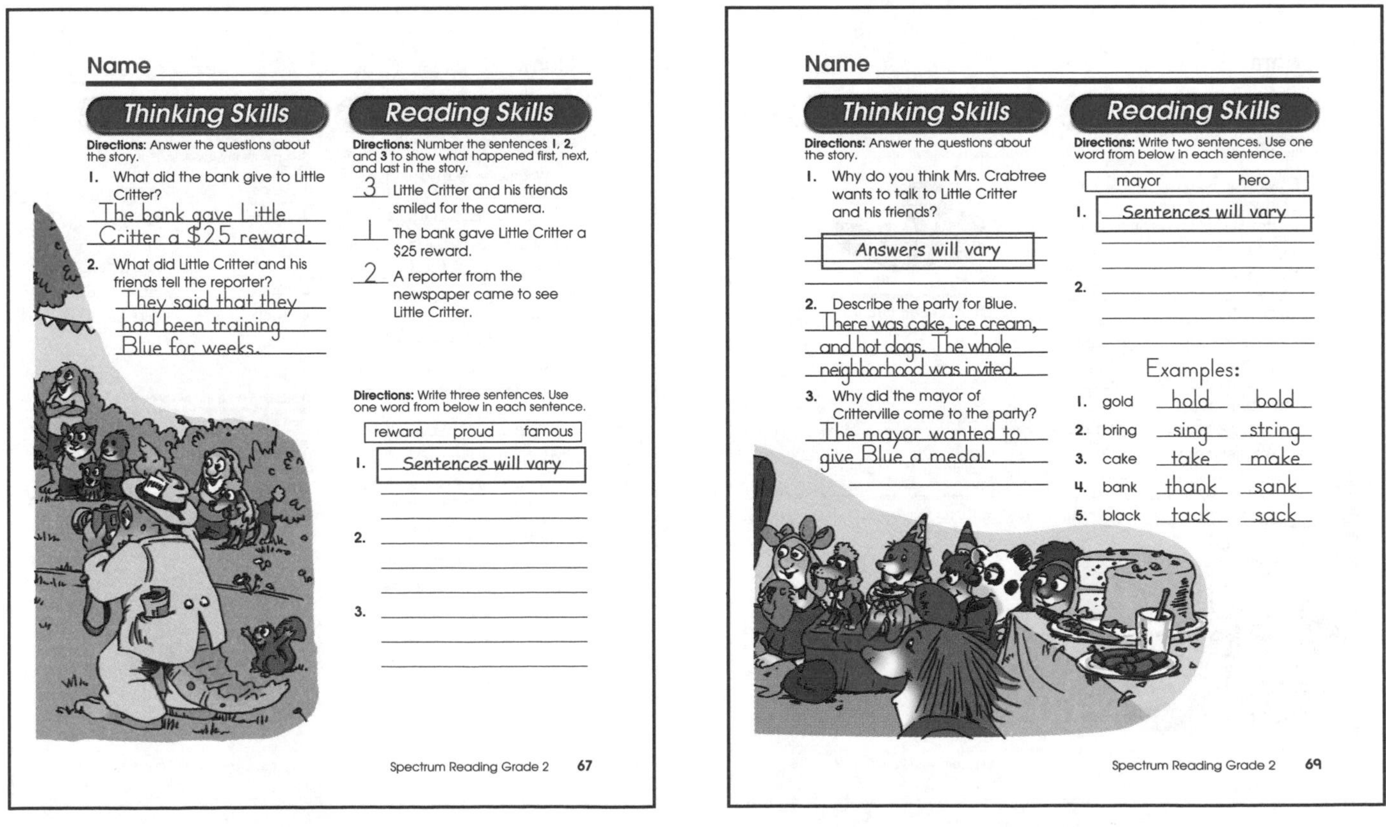

Name

Thinking Skills

Directions: Answer the questions about the story.

1. What did the bank give to Little Critter?
   The bank gave Little Critter a $25 reward.
2. What did Little Critter and his friends tell the reporter?
   They said that they had been training Blue for weeks.

Reading Skills

Directions: Number the sentences **1**, **2**, and **3** to show what happened first, next, and last in the story.

3 Little Critter and his friends smiled for the camera.
1 The bank gave Little Critter a $25 reward.
2 A reporter from the newspaper came to see Little Critter.

Directions: Write three sentences. Use one word from below in each sentence.

reward	proud	famous

1. Sentences will vary
2.
3.

Spectrum Reading Grade 2 67

Name

Thinking Skills

Directions: Answer the questions about the story.

1. Why do you think Mrs. Crabtree wants to talk to Little Critter and his friends?
   Answers will vary
2. Describe the party for Blue.
   There was cake, ice cream, and hot dogs. The whole neighborhood was invited.
3. Why did the mayor of Critterville come to the party?
   The mayor wanted to give Blue a medal.

Reading Skills

Directions: Write two sentences. Use one word from below in each sentence.

mayor	hero

1. Sentences will vary
2.

Examples:

1. gold — hold, bold
2. bring — sing, string
3. cake — take, make
4. bank — thank, sank
5. black — tack, sack

Spectrum Reading Grade 2 69

Answer Key

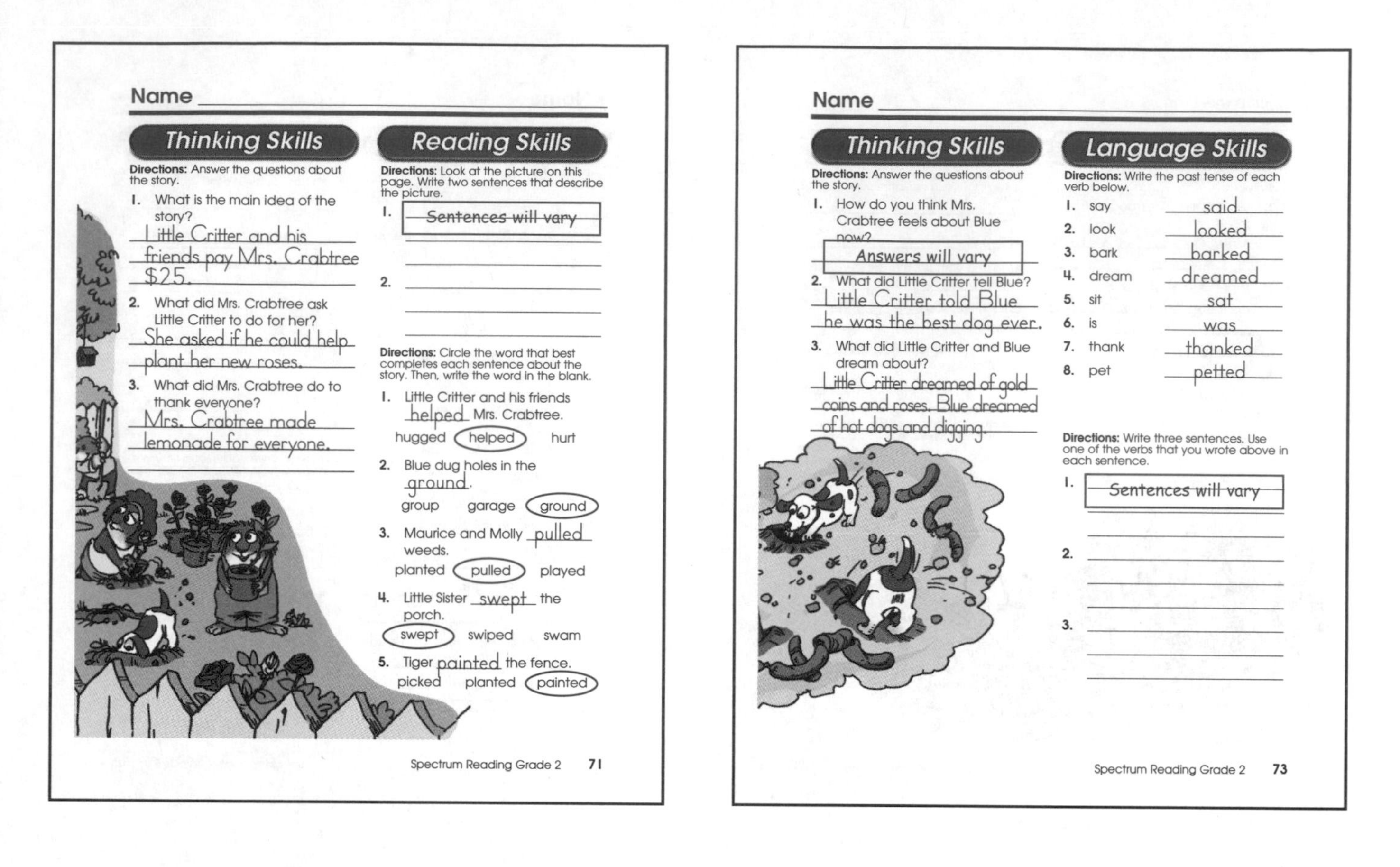

Name

Thinking Skills

Directions: Answer the questions about the story.

1. What is the main idea of the story?
   Little Critter and his friends pay Mrs. Crabtree $25.
2. What did Mrs. Crabtree ask Little Critter to do for her?
   She asked if he could help plant her new roses.
3. What did Mrs. Crabtree do to thank everyone?
   Mrs. Crabtree made lemonade for everyone.

Reading Skills

Directions: Look at the picture on this page. Write two sentences that describe the picture.

1. Sentences will vary
2.

Directions: Circle the word that best completes each sentence about the story. Then, write the word in the blank.

1. Little Critter and his friends helped Mrs. Crabtree.
   hugged (helped) hurt
2. Blue dug holes in the ground.
   group garage (ground)
3. Maurice and Molly pulled weeds.
   planted (pulled) played
4. Little Sister swept the porch.
   (swept) swiped swam
5. Tiger painted the fence.
   picked planted (painted)

Spectrum Reading Grade 2 71

Name

Thinking Skills

Directions: Answer the questions about the story.

1. How do you think Mrs. Crabtree feels about Blue now?
   Answers will vary
2. What did Little Critter tell Blue?
   Little Critter told Blue he was the best dog ever.
3. What did Little Critter and Blue dream about?
   Little Critter dreamed of gold coins and roses. Blue dreamed of hot dogs and digging.

Language Skills

Directions: Write the past tense of each verb below.

1. say — said
2. look — looked
3. bark — barked
4. dream — dreamed
5. sit — sat
6. is — was
7. thank — thanked
8. pet — petted

Directions: Write three sentences. Use one of the verbs that you wrote above in each sentence.

1. Sentences will vary
2.
3.

Spectrum Reading Grade 2 73

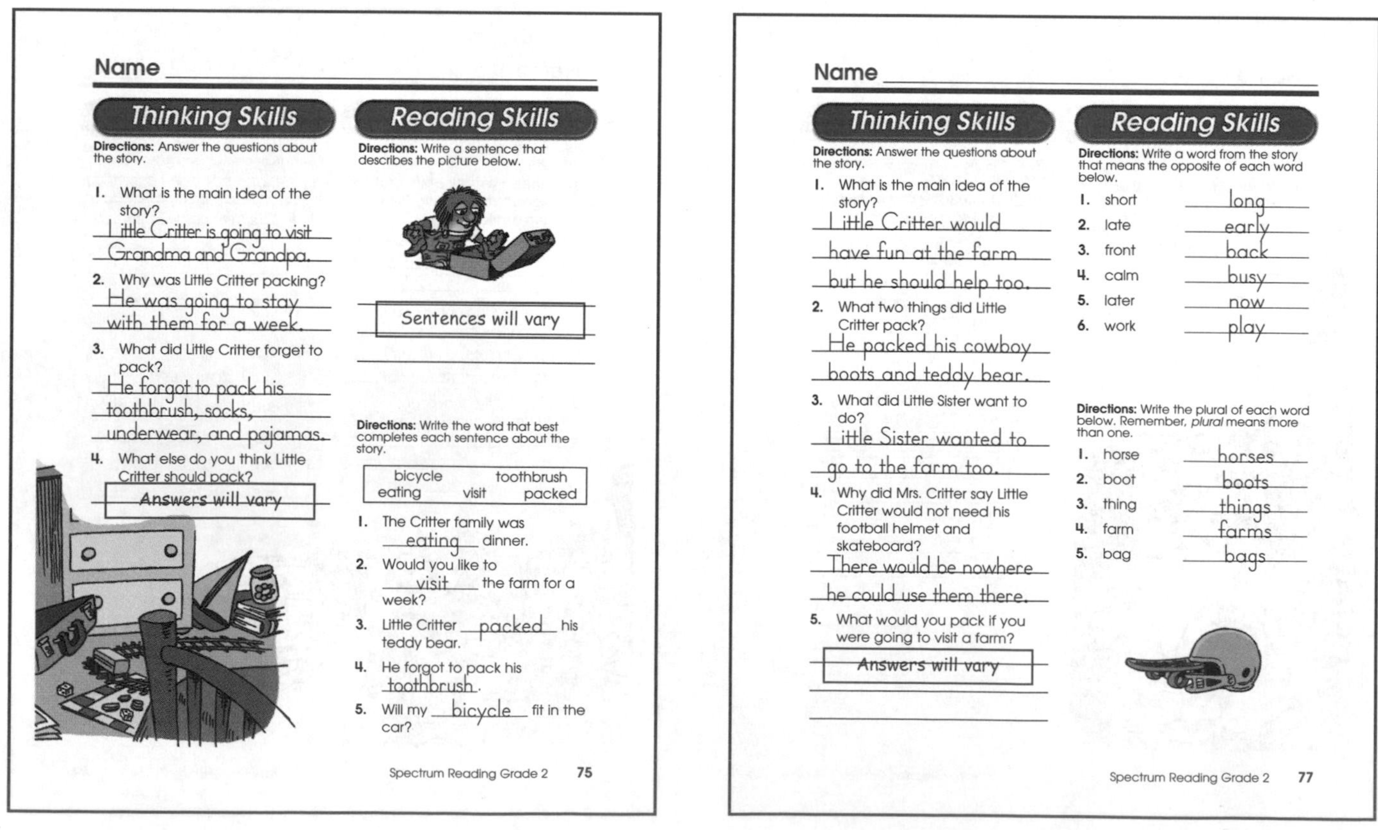

Name

Thinking Skills

Directions: Answer the questions about the story.

1. What is the main idea of the story?
   Little Critter is going to visit Grandma and Grandpa.
2. Why was Little Critter packing?
   He was going to stay with them for a week.
3. What did Little Critter forget to pack?
   He forgot to pack his toothbrush, socks, underwear, and pajamas.
4. What else do you think Little Critter should pack?
   Answers will vary

Reading Skills

Directions: Write a sentence that describes the picture below.

Sentences will vary

Directions: Write the word that best completes each sentence about the story.

bicycle toothbrush eating visit packed

1. The Critter family was eating dinner.
2. Would you like to visit the farm for a week?
3. Little Critter packed his teddy bear.
4. He forgot to pack his toothbrush.
5. Will my bicycle fit in the car?

Spectrum Reading Grade 2 75

Name

Thinking Skills

Directions: Answer the questions about the story.

1. What is the main idea of the story?
   Little Critter would have fun at the farm but he should help too.
2. What two things did Little Critter pack?
   He packed his cowboy boots and teddy bear.
3. What did Little Sister want to do?
   Little Sister wanted to go to the farm too.
4. Why did Mrs. Critter say Little Critter would not need his football helmet and skateboard?
   There would be nowhere he could use them there.
5. What would you pack if you were going to visit a farm?
   Answers will vary

Reading Skills

Directions: Write a word from the story that means the opposite of each word below.

1. short — long
2. late — early
3. front — back
4. calm — busy
5. later — now
6. work — play

Directions: Write the plural of each word below. Remember, *plural* means more than one.

1. horse — horses
2. boot — boots
3. thing — things
4. farm — farms
5. bag — bags

Spectrum Reading Grade 2 77

Answer Key

Name

Thinking Skills

Directions: Answer the questions about the story.

1. What is the main idea of the story?
It took a long time to get to Grandma and Grandpa's because Little Sister had to use the bathroom.
2. What did Little Sister try to do?
She tried to bring her suitcase.
3. What two stops did Mr. Critter make?
They stopped at a gas station.
4. Describe what the Critter family saw on their drive.
They saw fewer buildings and houses and more green fields.
5. Why was Little Critter upset?
He thought they were never going to get to the farm.

Reading Skills

Directions: Write each group of words from the story in **ABC** order.

1. morning, stop, gas, can — can, gas, morning, stop
2. farm, soon, took, houses — farm, houses, soon, took

Language Skills

Directions: Circle the verb that best completes each sentence about the story. Then, write the verb in the blank.

1. Little Critter buckled his seat belt.
buckling (buckled) buckle
2. Little Critter had to go to the bathroom.
gone went (go)
3. Little Critter tapped Mom's shoulder.
tap (tapped) tapping
4. Dad drove the car to the farm.
drive driven (drove)

Spectrum Reading Grade 2 79

Name

Thinking Skills

Directions: Answer the questions about the story.

1. What did the Critter family have for dessert?
They had cake for dessert.
2. What did Little Critter do to help?
He cleared the table, then started washing the dishes.
3. What flowed from the sink?
Soap bubbles flowed from the sink.
4. How do you think Little Critter felt when he was helping?
Answers will vary

Reading Skills

Directions: Write a word from the story that rhymes with each word below.

1. bunch — lunch
2. think — sink
3. wishes — dishes
4. growing — flowing
5. able — table

Directions: Write two sentences that describe how you help out at home.

1. Sentences will vary
2.

Language Skills

Directions: Write the past tense of each verb below.

1. clear — cleared
2. eat — ate
3. drink — drank
4. wipe — wiped
5. drop — dropped

Spectrum Reading Grade 2 81

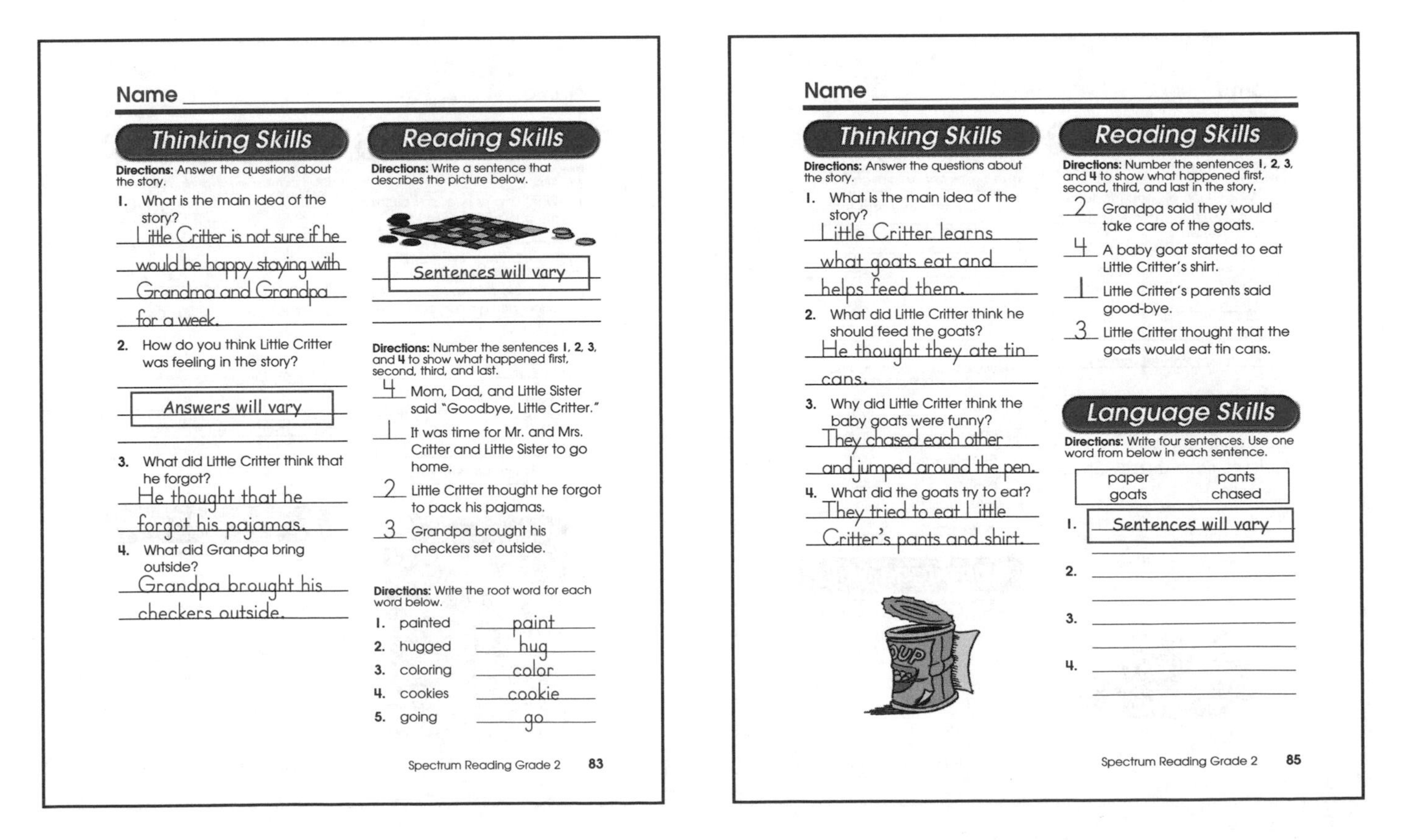

Name

Thinking Skills

Directions: Answer the questions about the story.

1. What is the main idea of the story?
Little Critter is not sure if he would be happy staying with Grandma and Grandpa for a week.
2. How do you think Little Critter was feeling in the story?
Answers will vary
3. What did Little Critter think that he forgot?
He thought that he forgot his pajamas.
4. What did Grandpa bring outside?
Grandpa brought his checkers outside.

Reading Skills

Directions: Write a sentence that describes the picture below.

Sentences will vary

Directions: Number the sentences **1**, **2**, **3**, and **4** to show what happened first, second, third, and last.

4 Mom, Dad, and Little Sister said "Goodbye, Little Critter."
1 It was time for Mr. and Mrs. Critter and Little Sister to go home.
2 Little Critter thought he forgot to pack his pajamas.
3 Grandpa brought his checkers set outside.

Directions: Write the root word for each word below.

1. painted — paint
2. hugged — hug
3. coloring — color
4. cookies — cookie
5. going — go

Spectrum Reading Grade 2 83

Name

Thinking Skills

Directions: Answer the questions about the story.

1. What is the main idea of the story?
Little Critter learns what goats eat and helps feed them.
2. What did Little Critter think he should feed the goats?
He thought they ate tin cans.
3. Why did Little Critter think the baby goats were funny?
They chased each other and jumped around the pen.
4. What did the goats try to eat?
They tried to eat Little Critter's pants and shirt.

Reading Skills

Directions: Number the sentences **1**, **2**, **3**, and **4** to show what happened first, second, third, and last in the story.

2 Grandpa said they would take care of the goats.
4 A baby goat started to eat Little Critter's shirt.
1 Little Critter's parents said good-bye.
3 Little Critter thought that the goats would eat tin cans.

Language Skills

Directions: Write four sentences. Use one word from below in each sentence.

paper, pants, goats, chased

1. Sentences will vary
2.
3.
4.

Spectrum Reading Grade 2 85

Answer Key

Name

Thinking Skills

Directions: Answer the questions about the story.

1. Why did Little Critter have trouble sleeping?
   Little Critter had trouble sleeping because he missed his family.
2. What did Grandma do to make Little Critter feel better?
   Grandma turned on the night light.
3. What did Grandma give to Little Critter?
   She gave him his teddy bear.
4. What did Grandpa do to help?
   He called Little Critter's family so that they could say "Good-night."

Reading Skills

Directions: Circle the word that best completes each sentence about the story. Then, write the word in the blank.

1. This bed is much bigger than my bed at home.
   smaller (bigger) nicer
2. Little Critter hugged his bear.
   lost threw (hugged)
3. Little Critter climbed into the bed.
   fell crawled (climbed)
4. Grandpa handed the telephone to Little Critter.
   sent (handed) ended
5. The room was much darker than Little Critter's room at home.
   (darker) older louder

Directions: Write a word from the story that rhymes with each word below.

1. boom room
2. moon soon
3. such much
4. burned turned
5. creep sleep
6. light night

Spectrum Reading Grade 2 87

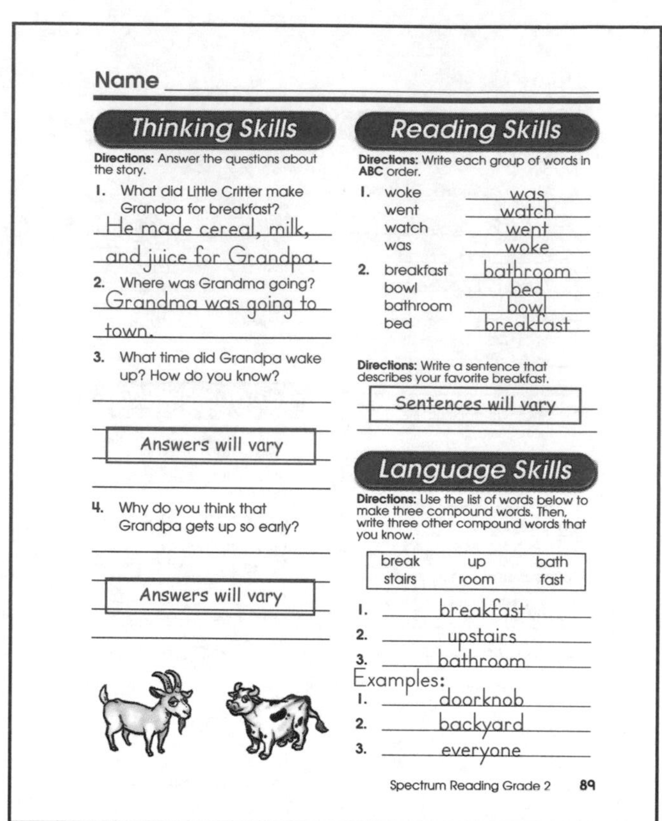

Name

Thinking Skills

Directions: Answer the questions about the story.

1. What did Little Critter make Grandpa for breakfast?
   He made cereal, milk, and juice for Grandpa.
2. Where was Grandma going?
   Grandma was going to town.
3. What time did Grandpa wake up? How do you know?
   Answers will vary
4. Why do you think that Grandpa gets up so early?
   Answers will vary

Reading Skills

Directions: Write each group of words in **ABC** order.

1. woke, went, watch, was — was, watch, went, woke
2. breakfast, bowl, bathroom, bed — bathroom, bed, bowl, breakfast

Directions: Write a sentence that describes your favorite breakfast.

Sentences will vary

Language Skills

Directions: Use the list of words below to make three compound words. Then, write three other compound words that you know.

break	up	bath
stairs	room	fast

1. breakfast
2. upstairs
3. bathroom

Examples:

1. doorknob
2. backyard
3. everyone

Spectrum Reading Grade 2 89

Name

Thinking Skills

Directions: Answer the questions about the story.

1. What is the pig slop made of?
   Pig slop is made from scraps in the kitchen.
2. List two things that Grandpa taught Little Critter about pigs.
   1. They have more babies than any other farm animal.
   2. They are very smart animals.
3. What else did Grandpa and Little Critter do for the pigs besides feed them?
   They gave them water to drink.
4. What do you think Grandpa and Little Critter will do next?
   Answers will vary

Reading Skills

Directions: Write three sentences that describe the picture on page 90.

1. Sentences will vary
2.
3.

Directions: Write a word from the story that means the opposite of each word below.

1. tiny enormous
2. on off
3. hard soft
4. warm cool
5. light heavy

Language Skills

Directions: Write a contraction from the story that stands for each pair of words.

1. they are they're
2. let us let's
3. that is that's

Spectrum Reading Grade 2 91

Name

Thinking Skills

Directions: Answer the questions about the story.

1. What time of year do you think the story takes place? Why?
   Answers will vary
2. What were Grandpa and Little Critter going to do after their swim?
   They were going to go back to work.
3. Would you like to swim in Grandpa's pond? Why or why not?
   Answers will vary

Reading Skills

Directions: Write a word from the story that has the same beginning blend as each word below.

1. fly floated
2. fry frog
3. grow great
4. swan swimming
5. step stuck

Directions: Write a sentence that describes the picture on this page.

Sentences will vary

Language Skills

Directions: Write the past tense of each verb below.

1. float floated
2. jump jumped
3. swim swam
4. paddle paddled
5. walk walked

Spectrum Reading Grade 2 93

Answer Key

Name

Thinking Skills

Directions: Answer the questions about the story.

1. What is the main idea of the story?
   Little Critter wanted to make lunch for Grandpa.
2. What did Little Critter make for lunch?
   He made peanut butter and pickle sandwiches with orange juice and potato chips.
3. How did Little Critter feel about making lunch for Grandpa?
   He was proud because he could do it all by himself.
4. Do you think Grandpa liked the lunch? Why or why not?
   Answers will vary

Reading Skills

Directions: Write two words from the story that have each vowel sound.

1. Long e need be
2. Short i did pickle
3. Short u lunch butter
4. Long i fine kind
5. Short e went get
6. Long a make came

Language Skills

Directions: Write three sentences. Use one word from below in each sentence.

famous delicious favorite

1. Sentences will vary
2.
3.

Spectrum Reading Grade 2 95

Name

Thinking Skills

Directions: Answer the questions about the story.

1. What is the main idea of the story?
   Little Critter helps Grandpa milk the cows.
2. What did Little Critter do while Grandpa milked Jody?
   He fed hay to her.
3. What kinds of foods are made from milk?
   Foods like cheese, butter, yogurt, and ice cream
4. How does a big farm do things differently?
   A big farm uses milking machines rather than doing it by hand.

Reading Skills

Directions: Write **F** next to the statements that are **facts** and **O** next to the statements that are **opinions**.

F 1. Cows have four stomachs.
O 2. Cows are the smartest animals in the world.
F 3. Cheese and yogurt can be made from milk.
O 4. Ice cream is the best snack.
F 5. Cows feed milk to their calves.
F 6. A mother cow makes extra milk.

Directions: Write three sentences that describe the picture on page 96.

1. Sentences will vary
2.
3.

Spectrum Reading Grade 2 97

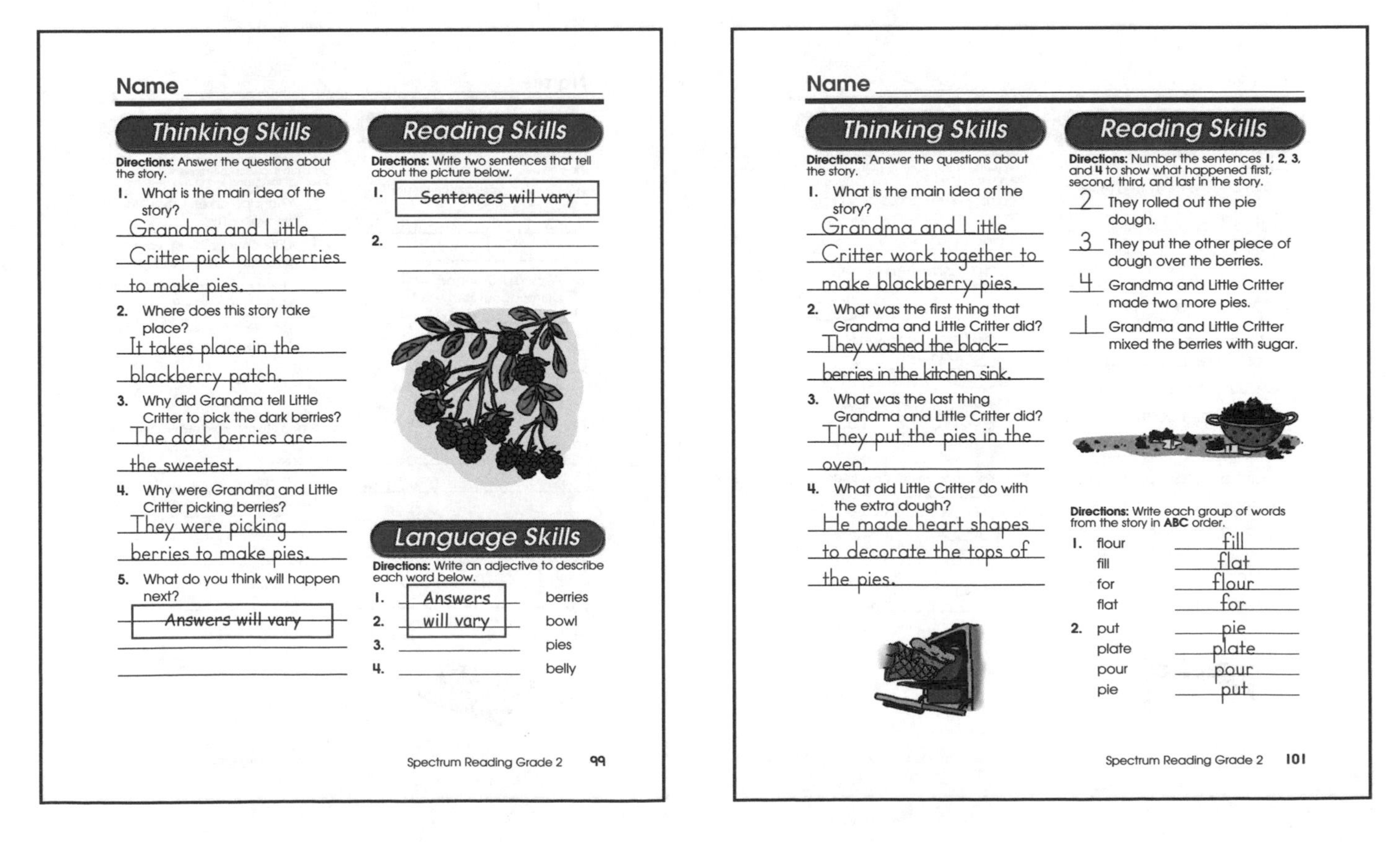

Name

Thinking Skills

Directions: Answer the questions about the story.

1. What is the main idea of the story?
   Grandma and Little Critter pick blackberries to make pies.
2. Where does this story take place?
   It takes place in the blackberry patch.
3. Why did Grandma tell Little Critter to pick the dark berries?
   The dark berries are the sweetest.
4. Why were Grandma and Little Critter picking berries?
   They were picking berries to make pies.
5. What do you think will happen next?
   Answers will vary

Reading Skills

Directions: Write two sentences that tell about the picture below.

1. Sentences will vary
2.

Language Skills

Directions: Write an adjective to describe each word below.

1. Answers will vary berries
2. bowl
3. pies
4. belly

Spectrum Reading Grade 2 99

Name

Thinking Skills

Directions: Answer the questions about the story.

1. What is the main idea of the story?
   Grandma and Little Critter work together to make blackberry pies.
2. What was the first thing that Grandma and Little Critter did?
   They washed the blackberries in the kitchen sink.
3. What was the last thing Grandma and Little Critter did?
   They put the pies in the oven.
4. What did Little Critter do with the extra dough?
   He made heart shapes to decorate the tops of the pies.

Reading Skills

Directions: Number the sentences **1**, **2**, **3**, and **4** to show what happened first, second, third, and last in the story.

2 They rolled out the pie dough.
3 They put the other piece of dough over the berries.
4 Grandma and Little Critter made two more pies.
1 Grandma and Little Critter mixed the berries with sugar.

Directions: Write each group of words from the story in **ABC** order.

1. flour, fill, for, flat — fill, flat, flour, for
2. put, plate, pour, pie — pie, plate, pour, put

Spectrum Reading Grade 2 101

Answer Key

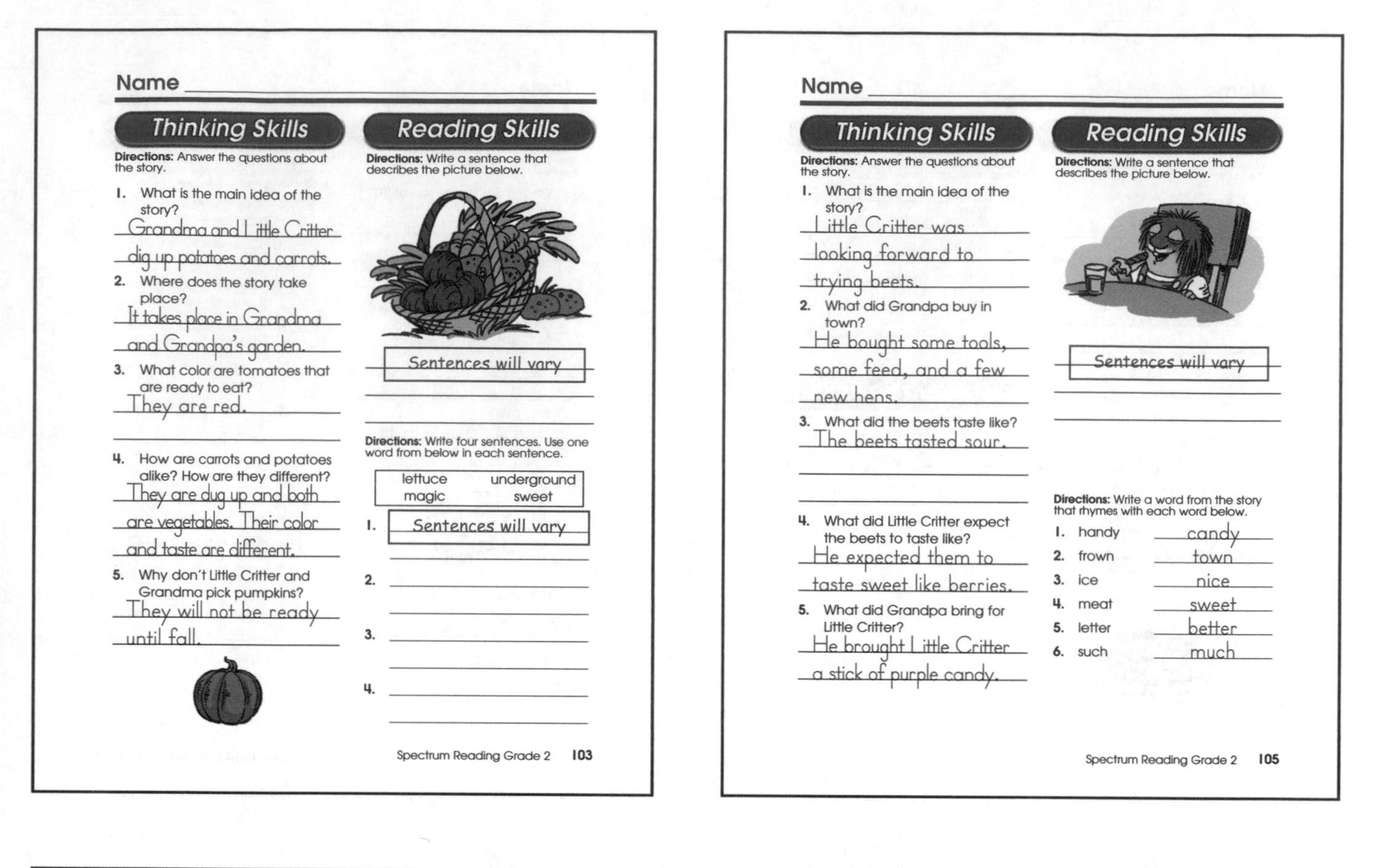

Name

Thinking Skills

Directions: Answer the questions about the story.

1. What is the main idea of the story?
   Grandma and Little Critter dig up potatoes and carrots.
2. Where does the story take place?
   It takes place in Grandma and Grandpa's garden.
3. What color are tomatoes that are ready to eat?
   They are red.
4. How are carrots and potatoes alike? How are they different?
   They are dug up and both are vegetables. Their color and taste are different.
5. Why don't Little Critter and Grandma pick pumpkins?
   They will not be ready until fall.

Reading Skills

Directions: Write a sentence that describes the picture below.

Sentences will vary

Directions: Write four sentences. Use one word from below in each sentence.

lettuce	underground
magic	sweet

1. Sentences will vary
2.
3.
4.

Spectrum Reading Grade 2 103

Name

Thinking Skills

Directions: Answer the questions about the story.

1. What is the main idea of the story?
   Little Critter was looking forward to trying beets.
2. What did Grandpa buy in town?
   He bought some tools, some feed, and a few new hens.
3. What did the beets taste like?
   The beets tasted sour.
4. What did Little Critter expect the beets to taste like?
   He expected them to taste sweet like berries.
5. What did Grandpa bring for Little Critter?
   He brought Little Critter a stick of purple candy.

Reading Skills

Directions: Write a sentence that describes the picture below.

Sentences will vary

Directions: Write a word from the story that rhymes with each word below.

1. handy candy
2. frown town
3. ice nice
4. meat sweet
5. letter better
6. such much

Spectrum Reading Grade 2 105

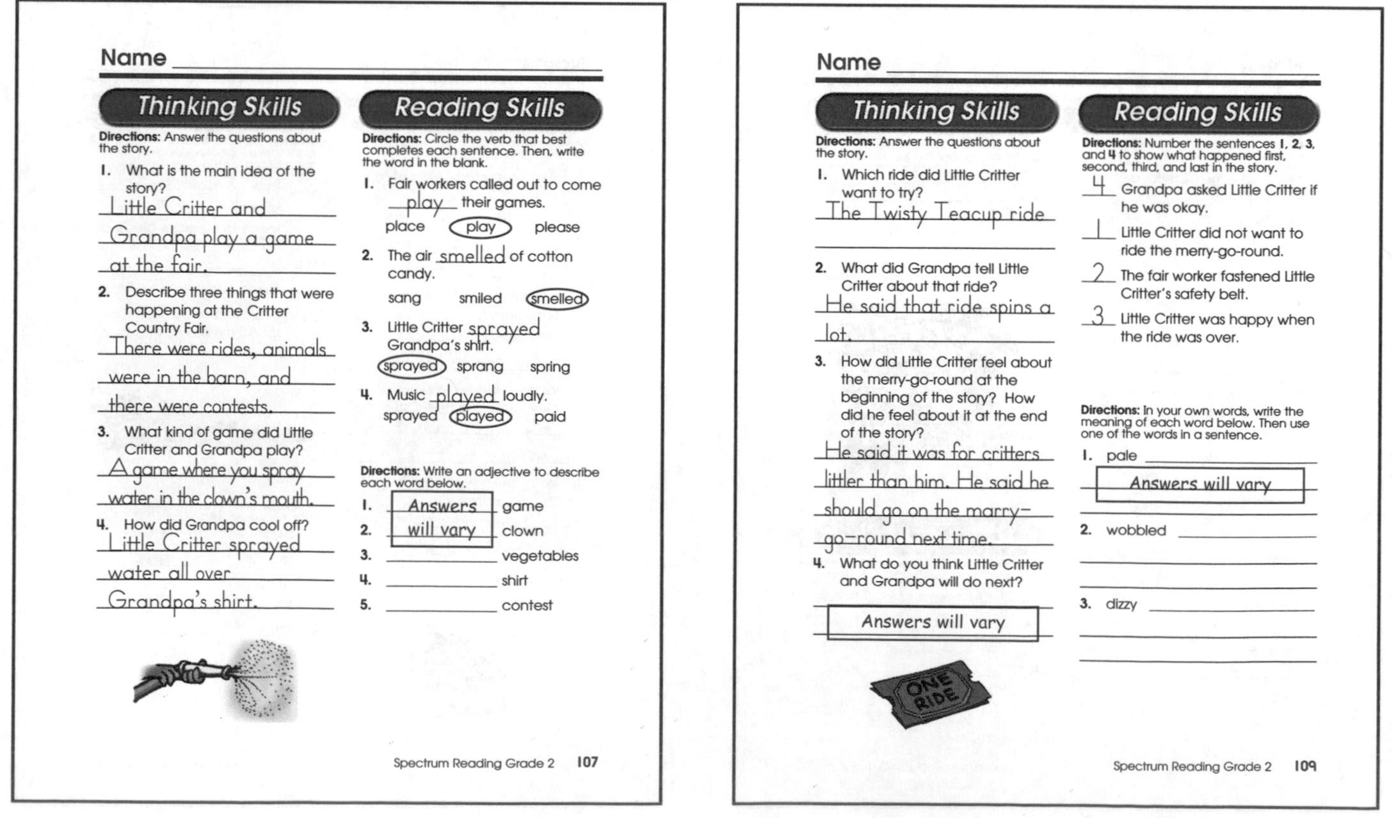

Name

Thinking Skills

Directions: Answer the questions about the story.

1. What is the main idea of the story?
   Little Critter and Grandpa play a game at the fair.
2. Describe three things that were happening at the Critter Country Fair.
   There were rides, animals were in the barn, and there were contests.
3. What kind of game did Little Critter and Grandpa play?
   A game where you spray water in the clown's mouth.
4. How did Grandpa cool off?
   Little Critter sprayed water all over Grandpa's shirt.

Reading Skills

Directions: Circle the verb that best completes each sentence. Then, write the word in the blank.

1. Fair workers called out to come play their games.
   place (play) please
2. The air smelled of cotton candy.
   sang smiled (smelled)
3. Little Critter sprayed Grandpa's shirt.
   (sprayed) sprang spring
4. Music played loudly.
   sprayed (played) paid

Directions: Write an adjective to describe each word below.

1. Answers will vary game
2. clown
3. vegetables
4. shirt
5. contest

Spectrum Reading Grade 2 107

Name

Thinking Skills

Directions: Answer the questions about the story.

1. Which ride did Little Critter want to try?
   The Twisty Teacup ride
2. What did Grandpa tell Little Critter about that ride?
   He said that ride spins a lot.
3. How did Little Critter feel about the merry-go-round at the beginning of the story? How did he feel about it at the end of the story?
   He said it was for critters littler than him. He said he should go on the merry-go-round next time.
4. What do you think Little Critter and Grandpa will do next?
   Answers will vary

Reading Skills

Directions: Number the sentences **1**, **2**, **3**, and **4** to show what happened first, second, third, and last in the story.

4 Grandpa asked Little Critter if he was okay.
1 Little Critter did not want to ride the merry-go-round.
2 The fair worker fastened Little Critter's safety belt.
3 Little Critter was happy when the ride was over.

Directions: In your own words, write the meaning of each word below. Then use one of the words in a sentence.

1. pale
   Answers will vary
2. wobbled
3. dizzy

Spectrum Reading Grade 2 109

Answer Key

Name

Thinking Skills

Directions: Answer the questions about the story.

1. What were the judges in the cooking tent doing?
They were tasting pies and making notes.
2. What contest did Little Critter join?
The pie-eating contest
3. How many pies did the winner eat?
The winner ate five pies.
4. How do you think Little Critter felt at the end of the story?
He felt rather sick.
5. Do you think Little Critter will eat the piece of pie Grandma saved for him? Why or why not?
Answers will vary

Reading Skills

Directions: Write each group of words in **ABC** order.

1. sign, stomach, saved, someone — saved, sign, someone, stomach
2. tent, tasting, their, table — table, tasting, tent, their
3. pie, please, placed, piece — pie, piece, placed, please
4. five, fur, faces, finish — faces, finish, five, fur

Directions: Write a sentence that describes the picture below.

Sentences will vary

Name

Thinking Skills

Directions: Answer the questions about the story.

1. What did Mom and Dad write in their letter to Little Critter?
They were glad Little Critter was having fun and was helping his grandparents.
2. How do you think Little Critter will feel when it is time to go home?
Answers will vary
3. Write three things that Little Critter could write about to his family.
Answers will vary
4. What does a "P.S." mean at the end of a letter?
It means "post script." It is added when the writer thinks of something else.

Reading Skills

Directions: Circle the word that best completes each sentence. Then, write the word in the blank.

1. They found a letter in the mailbox.
bound hound (found)
2. We are glad that you are having fun at the farm.
being (having) seeing
3. Little Sister liked the elephants best.
licked looked (liked)
4. We will see you in a couple of days.
saw seeing (see)
5. The weather has been very warm.
(been) seen was

Language Skills

Directions: Write two sentences. Use one word from below in each sentence.

found weather

1. Sentences will vary
2.

Name

Thinking Skills

Directions: Answer the questions about the story.

1. Where does this story take place?
It takes place in Little Critter's room.
2. How do you know that Little Critter was afraid of the thunderstorm?
Answers will vary
3. How did Grandpa help Little Critter?
He told Little Critter he had been afraid of thunderstorms when he was little.
4. What do you think Little Critter will do the next time there is a thunderstorm?
Answers will vary

Reading Skills

Directions: Number the sentences **1**, **2**, **3**, and **4** to show what happened first, second, third, and last in the story.

2 Little Critter dove under the bed.
1 There was a loud crash of thunder.
4 Little Critter wasn't scared anymore.
3 Grandpa told Little Critter a story.

Directions: Write a word from the story that rhymes with each word below.

1. mashed — flashed
2. race — face
3. hall — call
4. main — rain
5. sound — found
6. seed — need
7. mow — grow
8. sitting — hitting

Name

Thinking Skills

Directions: Answer the questions about the story.

1. What is the main idea of the story?
Grandpa teaches Little Critter some facts about horses and how to ride them.
2. List three things that Little Critter and Grandpa did for the horses.
They fed the horses hay.
They cleaned out their stalls.
They brushed their coats.
3. Why do horses wear horseshoes?
Horses wear horseshoes to protect their feet.
4. Would you rather ride Old Kicker or Buttercup? Why?
Answers will vary

Reading Skills

Directions: Write three sentences. Use one word from below in each sentence.

hooves exercise steer

1. Sentences will vary
2.
3.

Language Skills

Directions: Write the past tense of each verb below.

1. clean — cleaned
2. feed — fed
3. brush — brushed
4. say — said
5. pet — petted
6. call — called
7. name — named
8. wear — wore

Answer Key

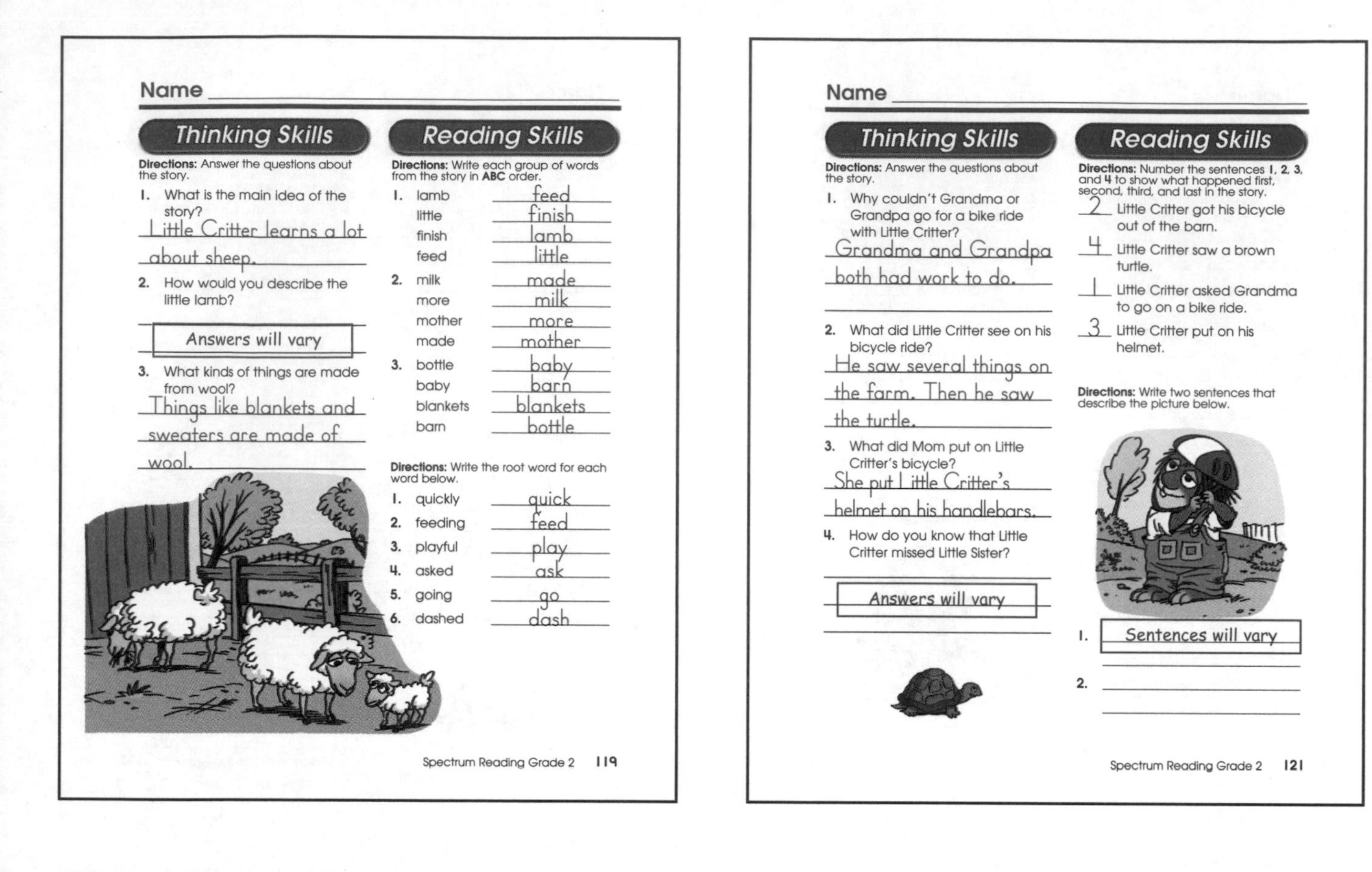

Name ______

Thinking Skills

Directions: Answer the questions about the story.

1. What is the main idea of the story?
   Little Critter learns a lot about sheep.
2. How would you describe the little lamb?
   Answers will vary
3. What kinds of things are made from wool?
   Things like blankets and sweaters are made of wool.

Reading Skills

Directions: Write each group of words from the story in **ABC** order.

	Words	Answer
1.	lamb	feed
	little	finish
	finish	lamb
	feed	little
2.	milk	made
	more	milk
	mother	more
	made	mother
3.	bottle	baby
	baby	barn
	blankets	blankets
	barn	bottle

Directions: Write the root word for each word below.

1. quickly — quick
2. feeding — feed
3. playful — play
4. asked — ask
5. going — go
6. dashed — dash

Spectrum Reading Grade 2 119

Name ______

Thinking Skills

Directions: Answer the questions about the story.

1. Why couldn't Grandma or Grandpa go for a bike ride with Little Critter?
   Grandma and Grandpa both had work to do.
2. What did Little Critter see on his bicycle ride?
   He saw several things on the farm. Then he saw the turtle.
3. What did Mom put on Little Critter's bicycle?
   She put Little Critter's helmet on his handlebars.
4. How do you know that Little Critter missed Little Sister?
   Answers will vary

Reading Skills

Directions: Number the sentences **1**, **2**, **3**, and **4** to show what happened first, second, third, and last in the story.

2 Little Critter got his bicycle out of the barn.
4 Little Critter saw a brown turtle.
1 Little Critter asked Grandma to go on a bike ride.
3 Little Critter put on his helmet.

Directions: Write two sentences that describe the picture below.

1. Sentences will vary
2. ______

Spectrum Reading Grade 2 121

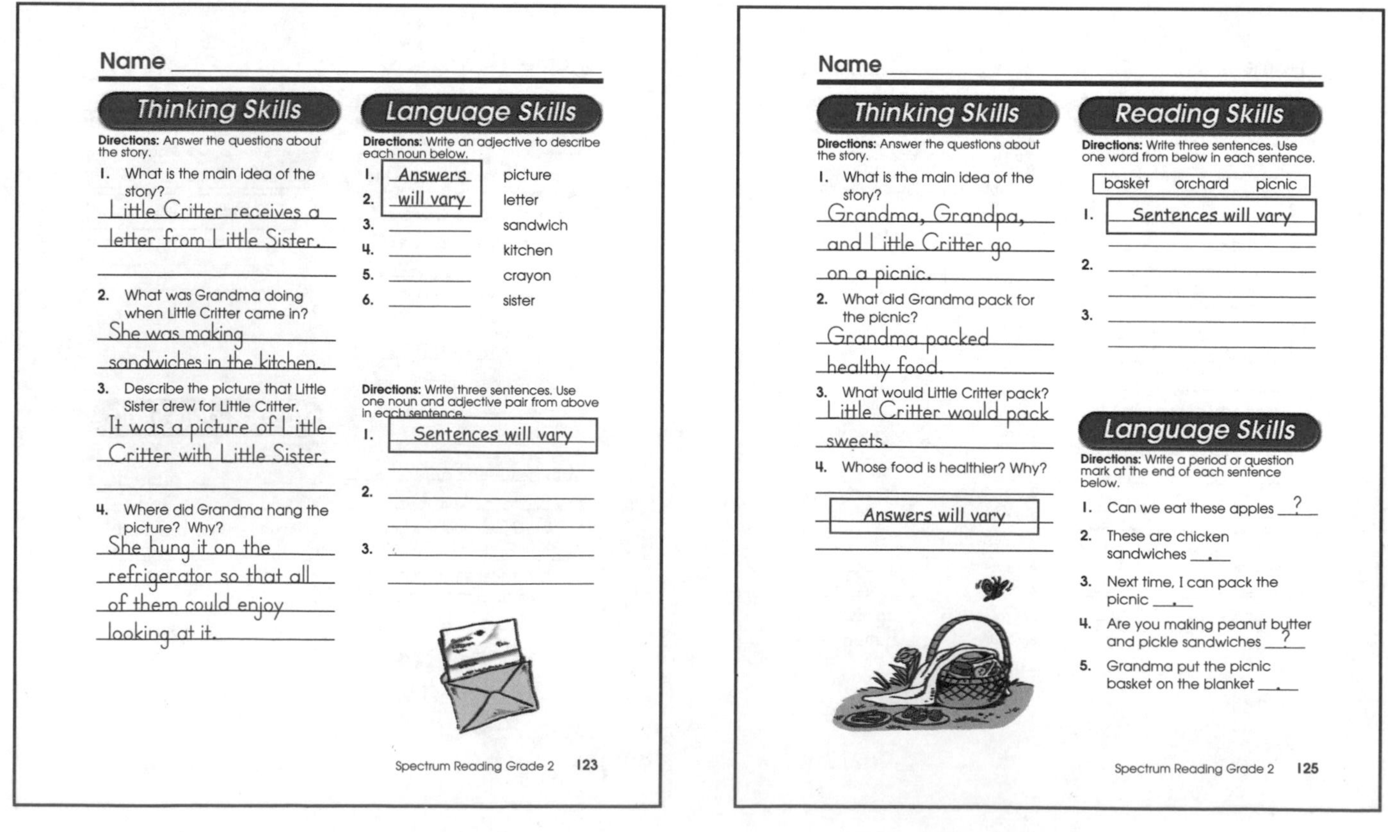

Name ______

Thinking Skills

Directions: Answer the questions about the story.

1. What is the main idea of the story?
   Little Critter receives a letter from Little Sister.
2. What was Grandma doing when Little Critter came in?
   She was making sandwiches in the kitchen.
3. Describe the picture that Little Sister drew for Little Critter.
   It was a picture of Little Critter with Little Sister.
4. Where did Grandma hang the picture? Why?
   She hung it on the refrigerator so that all of them could enjoy looking at it.

Language Skills

Directions: Write an adjective to describe each noun below.

1. Answers — picture
2. will vary — letter
3. ______ sandwich
4. ______ kitchen
5. ______ crayon
6. ______ sister

Directions: Write three sentences. Use one noun and adjective pair from above in each sentence.

1. Sentences will vary
2. ______
3. ______

Spectrum Reading Grade 2 123

Name ______

Thinking Skills

Directions: Answer the questions about the story.

1. What is the main idea of the story?
   Grandma, Grandpa, and Little Critter go on a picnic.
2. What did Grandma pack for the picnic?
   Grandma packed healthy food.
3. What would Little Critter pack?
   Little Critter would pack sweets.
4. Whose food is healthier? Why?
   Answers will vary

Reading Skills

Directions: Write three sentences. Use one word from below in each sentence.

basket orchard picnic

1. Sentences will vary
2. ______
3. ______

Language Skills

Directions: Write a period or question mark at the end of each sentence below.

1. Can we eat these apples ?
2. These are chicken sandwiches .
3. Next time, I can pack the picnic .
4. Are you making peanut butter and pickle sandwiches ?
5. Grandma put the picnic basket on the blanket .

Spectrum Reading Grade 2 125

Answer Key

Name

Thinking Skills

Directions: Answer the questions about the story.

1. Why did Grandpa think they needed to make a scarecrow?
   Because black birds were eating their corn.
2. What did Grandpa and Little Critter use to make the scarecrow?
   They used hay to stuff old clothes and tied everything together and put it on a wooden pole.
3. What did Little Critter think of the scarecrow?
   Little Critter thought it was the meanest, scariest scarcrow ever.

Reading Skills

Directions: Number the sentences **1**, **2**, **3**, and **4** to show what happened first, second, third, and last in the story.

3 Grandpa and Little Critter put the scarecrow in the cornfield.

1 Black birds were in the field eating corn.

4 Little Critter told the crows to watch out.

2 Grandpa and Little Critter decided to make a scarecrow.

Directions: Write a word from the story that rhymes with each word below.

1. day — hay
2. knows — crows
3. wink — think
4. while — smile
5. rack — black
6. horn — corn
7. feed — need
8. hole — pole

Spectrum Reading Grade 2 127

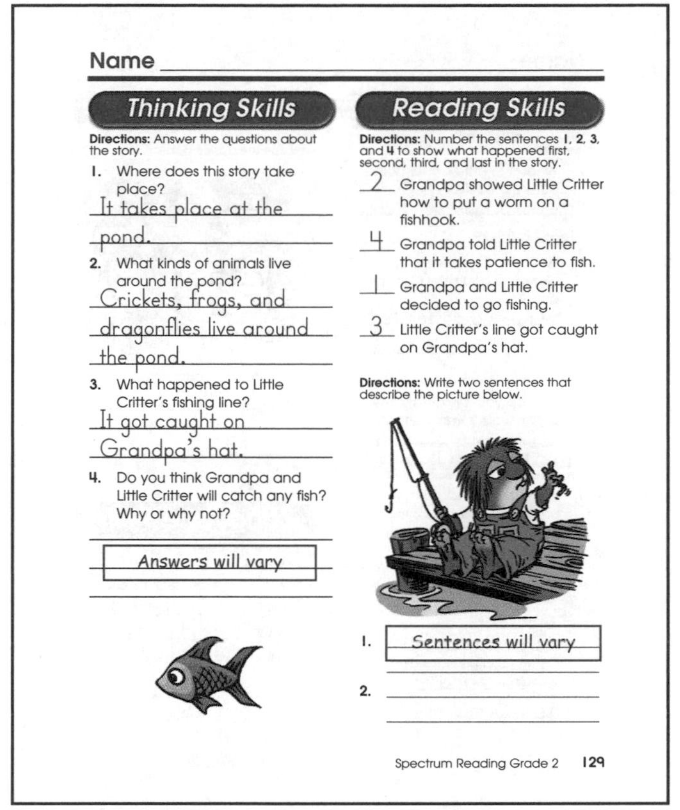

Name

Thinking Skills

Directions: Answer the questions about the story.

1. Where does this story take place?
   It takes place at the pond.
2. What kinds of animals live around the pond?
   Crickets, frogs, and dragonflies live around the pond.
3. What happened to Little Critter's fishing line?
   It got caught on Grandpa's hat.
4. Do you think Grandpa and Little Critter will catch any fish? Why or why not?
   Answers will vary

Reading Skills

Directions: Number the sentences **1**, **2**, **3**, and **4** to show what happened first, second, third, and last in the story.

2 Grandpa showed Little Critter how to put a worm on a fishhook.

4 Grandpa told Little Critter that it takes patience to fish.

1 Grandpa and Little Critter decided to go fishing.

3 Little Critter's line got caught on Grandpa's hat.

Directions: Write two sentences that describe the picture below.

1. Sentences will vary
2.

Spectrum Reading Grade 2 129

Name

Thinking Skills

Directions: Answer the questions about the story.

1. What is the main idea of the story?
   Grandpa and Little Critter go to town and visit the general store.
2. What things did Little Critter think about buying?
   He thought about buying candy, a kite, or a yo-yo.
3. Describe the marbles that Little Critter bought.
   He bought a speckled blue one, a clear one, an orange-and-green one, and a red one.
4. How much did the marbles cost?
   The marbles cost one dollar.
5. What would you have bought at the general store? Why?
   Answers will vary

Reading Skills

Directions: Write two sentences that describe the picture below.

1. Sentences will vary
2.

Directions: Circle the word that best completes each sentence about the story. Then, write each word in the blank.

1. Grandma gave Little Critter four quarters.
   quarts queens (quarters)
2. Little Critter felt the smooth, shiny marbles.
   kites (marbles) candles
3. Grandma told Little Critter to buy a treat.
   (treat) trick trap

Spectrum Reading Grade 2 131

Name

Thinking Skills

Directions: Answer the questions about the story.

1. What is the main idea of the story?
   Little Critter will miss Grandma and Grandpa, but he is looking forward to going home.
2. What was Grandpa doing?
   Grandpa was taking a nap on the couch.
3. What was Grandma doing?
   Grandma was sewing.
4. What was Little Critter thinking as he wandered upstairs?
   He would miss Grandma and Grandpa, but he would be glad to be home.
5. What did Little Critter make for Grandma and Grandpa? Why?
   He made a card for them. He wanted to let them know that he had a good time there.

Reading Skills

Directions: Write two sentences that describe the picture below.

1. Sentences will vary
2.

Directions: Write a word from the story that rhymes with each word below.

1. measure — treasure
2. hard — card
3. door — floor
4. skies — pies
5. kiss — miss
6. sand — hand
7. making — baking

Spectrum Reading Grade 2 133

Answer Key

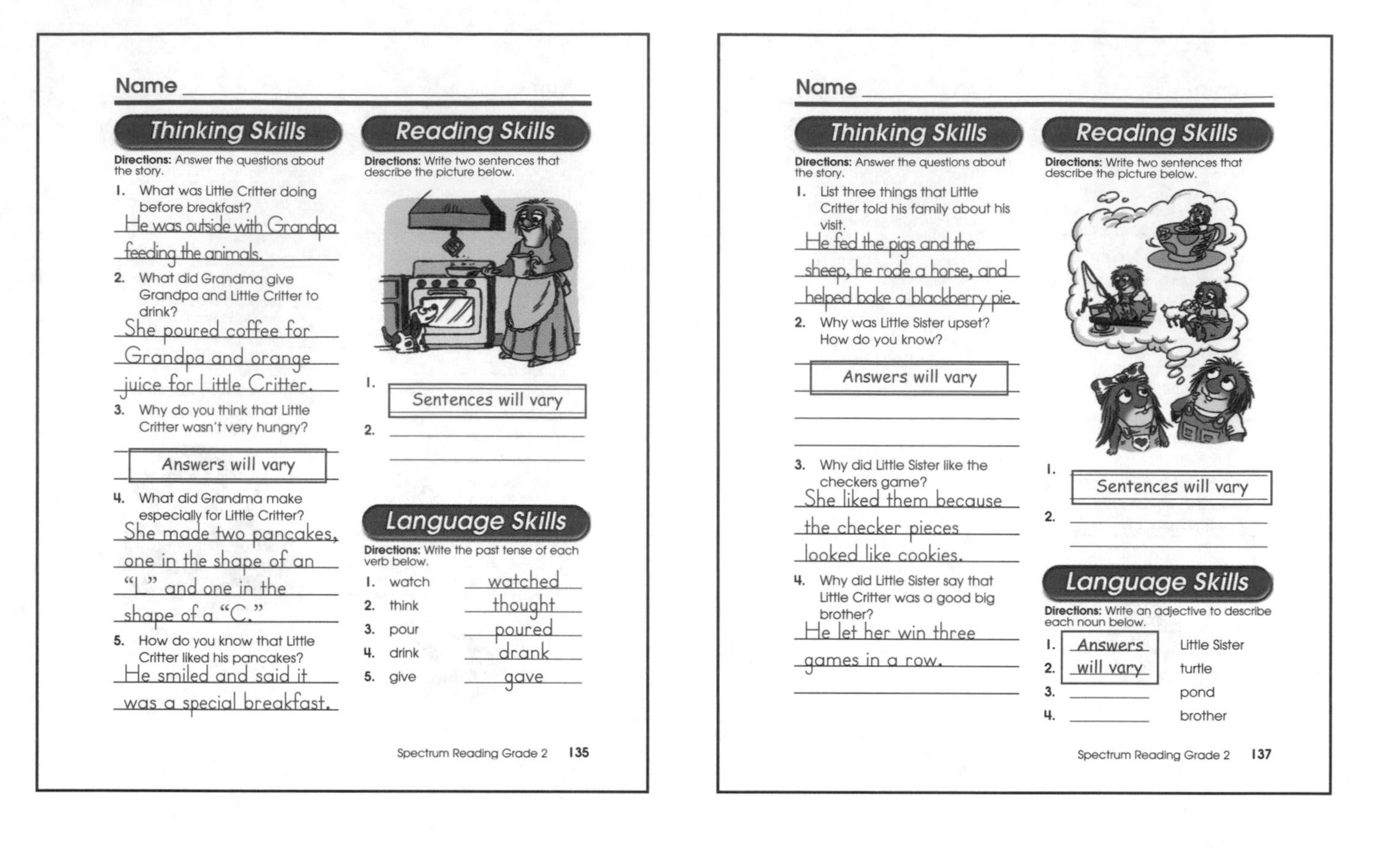

Name

Thinking Skills

Directions: Answer the questions about the story.

1. What was Little Critter doing before breakfast?
He was outside with Grandpa feeding the animals.
2. What did Grandma give Grandpa and Little Critter to drink?
She poured coffee for Grandpa and orange juice for Little Critter.
3. Why do you think that Little Critter wasn't very hungry?
Answers will vary
4. What did Grandma make especially for Little Critter?
She made two pancakes, one in the shape of an "L" and one in the shape of a "C."
5. How do you know that Little Critter liked his pancakes?
He smiled and said it was a special breakfast.

Reading Skills

Directions: Write two sentences that describe the picture below.

1. Sentences will vary
2.

Language Skills

Directions: Write the past tense of each verb below.

1. watch — watched
2. think — thought
3. pour — poured
4. drink — drank
5. give — gave

Spectrum Reading Grade 2 135

Name

Thinking Skills

Directions: Answer the questions about the story.

1. List three things that Little Critter told his family about his visit.
He fed the pigs and the sheep, he rode a horse, and helped bake a blackberry pie.
2. Why was Little Sister upset? How do you know?
Answers will vary
3. Why did Little Sister like the checkers game?
She liked them because the checker pieces looked like cookies.
4. Why did Little Sister say that Little Critter was a good big brother?
He let her win three games in a row.

Reading Skills

Directions: Write two sentences that describe the picture below.

1. Sentences will vary
2.

Language Skills

Directions: Write an adjective to describe each noun below.

1. Answers — Little Sister
2. will vary — turtle
3. — pond
4. — brother

Spectrum Reading Grade 2 137

Name

Thinking Skills

Directions: Answer the questions about the story.

1. What is the main idea of the story?
Little Critter said good-bye to all the animals as he was getting ready to leave.
2. Who will visit the farm next time?
Little Sister will visit the farm next time.
3. Why was Little Critter sad?
He was going to miss Grandma and Grandpa and the farm.
4. How did Little Critter remember his good manners?
He remembered to thank Grandpa and Grandma for everything.

Reading Skills

Directions: Write each group of words in **ABC** order.

1. then, they, thank, those, think — thank, then, they, think, those
2. sheep, said, she, so, sad — sad, said, she, sheep, so
3. head, home, him, hugged, his — head, him, his, home, hugged

Language Skills

Directions: Write a contraction from the story that stands for each pair of words below.

1. do not — don't
2. can not — can't
3. that is — that's

Spectrum Reading Grade 2 139

Name

Thinking Skills

Directions: Answer the questions about the story.

1. What did Little Critter do when he got home from the farm?
He went to his room.
2. What did Little Critter dream about?
He dreamed about green and yellow cornfields, lambs, blackberry pie, and pancakes.
3. How did Little Critter feel about being in his own room?
He was glad to see his own bed and toys.

Reading Skills

Directions: Number the sentences **1**, **2**, **3**, and **4** to show what happened first, second, third, and last in the story.

4 Little Critter said he could sleep in.
3 Little Critter dreamed about the farm.
1 Little Critter went right to his room.
2 Dad said that they all missed Little Critter.

Directions: Write four sentences. Use one word from below in each sentence.

animals dreamed costume remind

1. Sentences will vary
2.
3.
4.

Spectrum Reading Grade 2 141

Notes

Notes